PEOPLE OF
THE ICE AND SNOW

✛

TIME® **LIFE** BOOKS

Other Publications:

WEIGHT WATCHERS® SMART CHOICE RECIPE COLLECTION
TRUE CRIME
THE ART OF WOODWORKING
LOST CIVILIZATIONS
ECHOES OF GLORY
THE NEW FACE OF WAR
HOW THINGS WORK
WINGS OF WAR
CREATIVE EVERYDAY COOKING
COLLECTOR'S LIBRARY OF THE UNKNOWN
CLASSICS OF WORLD WAR II
TIME-LIFE LIBRARY OF CURIOUS AND UNUSUAL FACTS
AMERICAN COUNTRY
VOYAGE THROUGH THE UNIVERSE
THE THIRD REICH
THE TIME-LIFE GARDENER'S GUIDE
MYSTERIES OF THE UNKNOWN
TIME FRAME
FIX IT YOURSELF
FITNESS, HEALTH & NUTRITION
SUCCESSFUL PARENTING
HEALTHY HOME COOKING
UNDERSTANDING COMPUTERS
LIBRARY OF NATIONS
THE ENCHANTED WORLD
THE KODAK LIBRARY OF CREATIVE PHOTOGRAPHY
GREAT MEALS IN MINUTES
THE CIVIL WAR
PLANET EARTH
COLLECTOR'S LIBRARY OF THE CIVIL WAR
THE EPIC OF FLIGHT
THE GOOD COOK
WORLD WAR II
HOME REPAIR AND IMPROVEMENT
THE OLD WEST

For information on and a full description of any of the
Time-Life Books series listed above, please call
1-800-621-7026 or write:
Reader Information
Time-Life Customer Service
P.O. Box C-32068
Richmond, Virginia 23261-2068

This volume is one of a series that chronicles the history and culture of the Native Americans. Other books in the series include:

The Cover: Clad in a sealskin parka and armed with a rifle, an Eskimo from the town of Resolute on Cornwallis Island in the Northwest Territories prepares to set out for the hunt. Until recent times, the Eskimos had to rely on their skills as hunters and fishermen for survival in the cruel environment at the top of the world.

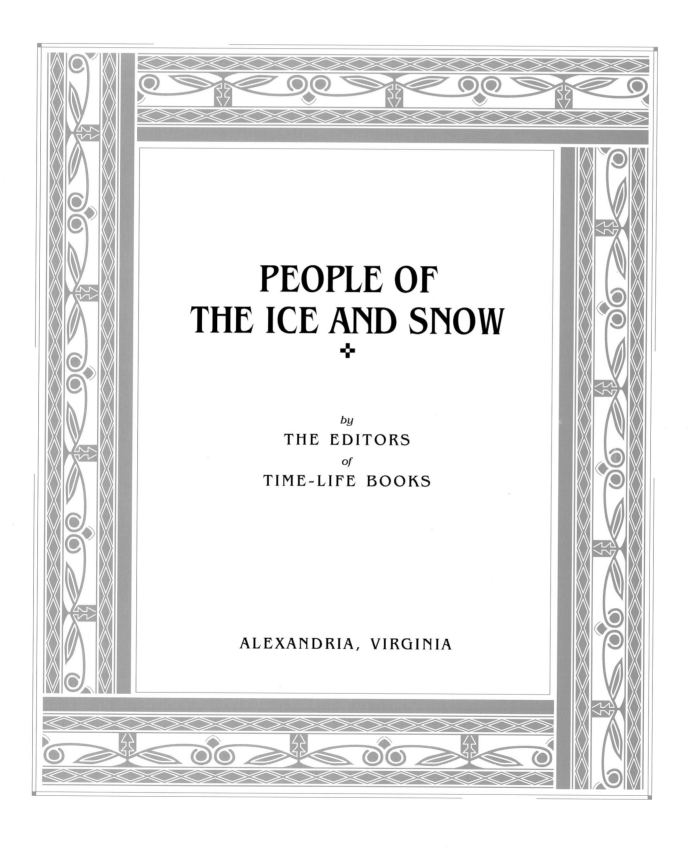

PEOPLE OF
THE ICE AND SNOW

✣

by
THE EDITORS
of
TIME-LIFE BOOKS

ALEXANDRIA, VIRGINIA

Time-Life Books is a division of TIME LIFE INC.

PRESIDENT and CEO: John M. Fahey Jr.
EDITOR-IN-CHIEF: John L. Papanek

TIME-LIFE BOOKS

MANAGING EDITOR: Roberta Conlan

Executive Art Director: Ellen Robling
Director of Photography and Research:
John Conrad Weiser
Senior Editors: Russell B. Adams Jr., Dale M. Brown,
Janet Cave, Lee Hassig, Robert Somerville,
Henry Woodhead
Director of Technology: Eileen Bradley
Director of Editorial Operations: Prudence G. Harris
Library: Louise D. Forstall

PRESIDENT: John D. Hall

Vice President, Director of Marketing:
Nancy K. Jones
Vice President, New Product Development:
Neil Kagan
Vice President, Book Production: Marjann Caldwell
Production Manager: Marlene Zack

THE AMERICAN INDIANS

SERIES EDITOR: Henry Woodhead
Administrative Editor: Loretta Y. Britten

Editorial Staff for *People of the Ice and Snow*
Senior Art Director: Ray Ripper
Picture Editor: Susan V. Kelly
Text Editors: John Newton (principal), Stephen G.
Hyslop, Stephanie Lewis
Associate Editors/Research-Writing: Trudy W.
Pearson (principal), Robert H. Wooldridge Jr.
Assistant Art Director: Susan M. Gibas
Senior Copyeditor: Ann Lee Bruen
Picture Coordinators: David Beard, Catherine Parrott
Editorial Assistant: Gemma Villanueva

Special Contributors: Ronald H. Bailey, Marfé
Ferguson Delano, Thomas Lewis, Susan Perry,
Lydia Preston, David S. Thomson, Gerald P. Tyson
(text); Martha Lee Beckington, Barbara Fleming,
Elizabeth Schleichert, Christine Soares, Marilyn
Murphy Terrell, Anne Whittle (research); Barbara L.
Klein (index).

Correspondents: Elisabeth Kraemer-Singh (Bonn),
Christine Hinze (London), Christina Lieberman
(New York), Maria Vincenza Aloisi (Paris), Ann
Natanson (Rome). Valuable assistance was also
provided by: Barbara Gevene Hertz (Copenhagen),
Daniel Donnelly (New York), Dag Christensen
(Oslo), Carolyn Sackett (Seattle).

First printing. Printed in U.S.A.
Published simultaneously in Canada.
School and library distribution by Time-Life
Education, P.O. Box 85026, Richmond, Virginia
23285-5026.
Time-Life is a trademark of Time Warner Inc. U.S.A.

Library of Congress Cataloging in Publication Data
People of the ice and snow / by the editors of Time-
Life Books.
    p. cm.—(The American Indians)
    Includes bibliographical references and index.
    ISBN 0-8094-9562-7
    l. Eskimos—Social life and customs. 2. Aleuts—
Social life and customs. 3. Arctic regions—Social
life and customs. I. Time-Life Books. II. Series.
E99.E7P346 1994   94-16653
979.8'004971—dc20   CIP

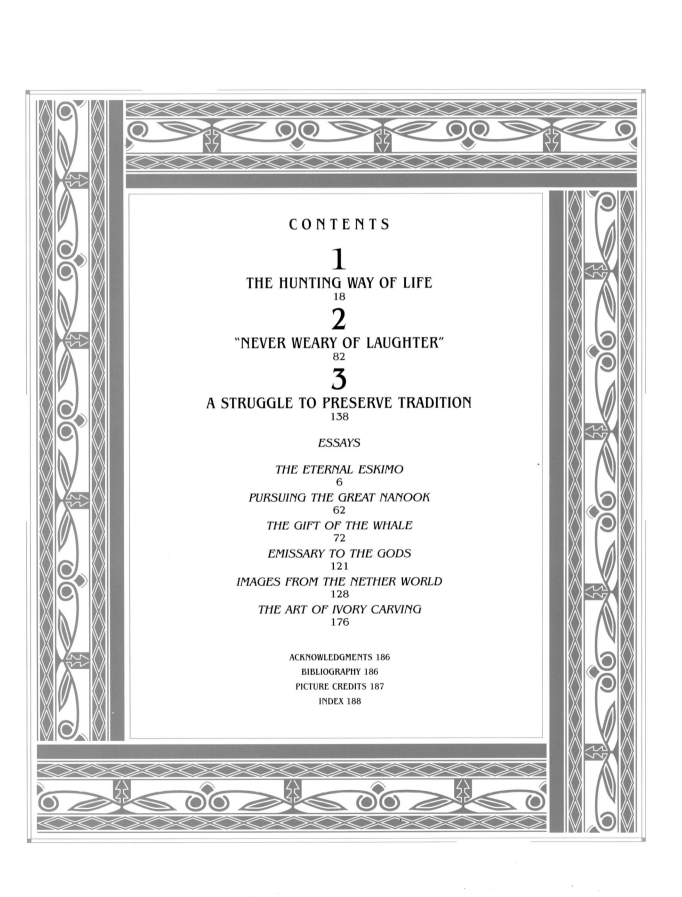

CONTENTS

THE ETERNAL ESKIMO

Isolated at the top of the world in a land of wild storms, eerie fogs, and winter darkness, the Eskimo peoples learned long ago how to find food, make shelter, and stay warm in places no other human beings dared to go. From Siberia to Greenland, generations grew up, formed families, spun legends, and lived out their lives as hunters, moving freely across ice, snow, and water in pursuit of the animals that provided them with food, clothing, tools, and weapons. The struggle for survival forged cultural values and a social order that sustain them even today in their fight to preserve their rich heritage—attributes that shine through these portraits, both early 20th century and contemporary, set against backdrops of their harsh and rugged land. "The whisperings of the Eskimo past mold the people of the Arctic as surely as does the cold starkness of their environment," a modern-day Inupiaq observed. "And it is to this past we must look to begin to understand them."

COUPLE WITH CHILD; KOTZEBUE SOUND, ALASKA

FAMILY; BARROW, ALASKA

MAN; KOBUK, ALASKA

MAN; BATHURST INLET, NORTHWEST TERRITORIES

GIRL AND PUPPY; SPENCE BAY, NORTHWEST TERRITORIES

GIRL AND PUPPY; KENT PENINSULA, NORTHWEST TERRITORIES

MAN; KING ISLAND, ALASKA

MAN; SARICHEF ISLAND, ALASKA

KAYAKER, KOTZEBUE SOUND, ALASKA

FATHER AND SON; BATHURST INLET, NORTHWEST TERRITORIES

WOMAN; SEWARD PENINSULA, ALASKA

WOMAN; NORTHWEST GREENLAND

1

THE HUNTING WAY OF LIFE

Concealed behind a shooting screen, a Greenlander aims his rifle at a dozing seal. When hunting with harpoons, Eskimos creep within throwing range with the help of scratchers made of seal claws (top left). Raking the device over the ice simulates the sound of a seal working at its breathing hole, lulling the animal.

Treeless and barren, buffeted by howling winds and surrounded by treacherous jumbles of ice for nine months of the year, the little spit of sand and gravel juts forlornly from the northwest coast of Alaska into the frigid waters of the Chukchi Sea. British ship captain Frederick Beechey, the first European to arrive at that remote spot, put ashore in 1826 and named the peninsula Point Hope in honor of a fellow Royal Navy officer, Vice Admiral Sir William Johnstone Hope. But the Inupiat Eskimos who have lived in this wind-scoured place for centuries—making it the oldest known settlement in Alaska—call it by a name descriptive of its distinctive shape: Tigara, or "index finger."

Like other indigenous peoples of the Arctic, the Tigaramiut, or "people of Tigara," depended almost entirely on hunting for their existence until well into the 20th century. Because of the cold, vegetation is limited to a few low flowering plants, mosses, lichens, and grass that appear during the short, cool summers and are of no importance as sustenance to humans. The Tigaramiut procured virtually all of their food, fuel, clothing, and tools from animals. "It seems as if nature carefully planned Tigara and worked out a system of spacing a succession of animals to be hunted," a modern-day Tigaramiut once observed, marveling at the seal, walrus, beluga whale, polar bear, tomcod, crab, caribou, fox, wolf, wolverine, lemming, squirrel, marmot, eider duck, auk, goose, gull, and other creatures that come every year—each in its season.

But at Tigara and other ancient Inupiat settlements dotting the Alaskan coast from Kingigin (Cape Prince of Wales) on the Bering Strait to Nuvuk (Barrow) on the Beaufort Sea section of the Arctic Ocean, one creature dominated the people's consciousness. At the core of their material and ceremonial culture was the bowhead whale, a behemoth that can weigh as much as 60 tons and grow to lengths of 60 feet and more. Each spring herds of as many as 50 of these leviathans swim past the native Alaskan villages on their annual migration from the Pacific Ocean to the plankton-rich waters at the edge of the polar icecap. In earlier times, the bowhead provided the Inupiat peoples with mountains of meat and blubber; barrels of oil for light and heat; great webs of baleen—the flexible, fern-like growths in the creature's mouth that allow it to strain seawater for food—for fishing lines, nets, and other equipment; and giant piles of bones that, in a land beyond the timberline, furnished the framework for boats, sleds, storage racks, grave markers, and the semisubterranean, sod-covered houses that served as permanent winter dwellings. In any given year, the successful pursuit of the bowhead made the difference between prosperity and poverty, famine and plenty.

Although the whaling season arrived in early spring, preparations began the previous autumn when the Tigaramiut returned from the summer caribou hunt in the tundra highlands to the east. As soon as the first slush ice appeared off the point, the community launched a succession of ceremonies, games, dances, and feasts that were as essential to the success of the whale hunt as the hunt itself. For the Tigaramiut and other native Alaskans, whaling was more than harvesting a resource for subsistence; it represented the sacred relationship between them and a world of spirits, supernatural human-animals, and charm powers that were as much a part of their reality as the ice and snow, and the very whales themselves.

The Tigaramiut are just one of countless small enclaves of Eskimos who live in a vast icy arc across the top of the globe. Taken together, the Eskimos—consisting of the Yupik and the Inupiat of Alaska and the Inuit of Canada and Greenland—along with their ancestral cousins, the Aleuts, represent the most widespread native population in the world. Their realm stretches from the Aleutian Islands and northeastern tip of Siberia in the west, through Alaska and northernmost Canada, and into Greenland in the east—a distance of more than 3,000 miles, far greater if the serrated coastlines become part of the calculation. Given the enormousness and the remoteness of their domain, it is not surprising that Eskimos were both the first and the last native North Americans to encounter Europeans. The first contact occurred early in the 11th century when Norse explorers established a temporary settlement on the northern end of Newfoundland. It was not until nearly a millennium later, in 1910, that a group of Inuits in the central Canadian Arctic, called Copper Eskimos by whites because of their use of unsmelted copper for tools, came upon members of a Canadian expedition.

When the Scottish explorer John Ross encountered the Avaner-suarmiut, or Polar Eskimos, in northwest Greenland in 1818, he reported

A herd of male walruses basks in the sun on the rocky shores of southwestern Alaska's Bristol Bay. The gregarious creatures served as an important source of meat and raw materials for the local Yupiks.

To announce the village feast marking the end of whaling season, Inupiat whalers danced from house to house wearing carved wooden masks like the one above. The black band that runs across the eyes signifies status.

that they considered themselves the only human beings on the earth. Yet despite their scattered distribution and extreme isolation, the arctic and the subarctic peoples remained remarkably uniform in language and lifestyle. Although climatic and topographical conditions created regional variations, the hunt remained the single most important activity in life. A man, his wife, and their children formed the basic social unit, and hereditary leaders did not exist. Instead, the greatest authority was vested in the ablest hunters, who often possessed shamanic power to communicate with the mysterious, all-pervasive spirits of the sky, the sea, and all things animate and inanimate.

Interestingly enough, relatively few Eskimos have inhabited the Arctic—the classic Eskimo setting where sea ice locks in the land for much of the year and only the top few inches of treeless tundra ever thaw. The conditions there are simply too harsh to support large societies of hunters and gatherers. Instead, the majority have lived in the evergreen forests and river valleys of southern Alaska, in the Yukon-Mackenzie country in the interior of Canada, and along the shores of the Alaska Peninsula, where the waters, warmed by Pacific currents, rarely freeze. By one conservative estimate, the Eskimo population in the 17th and 18th centuries was about 51,000, with perhaps no more than 10 percent living in the Arctic. Thus, many Eskimos never sheltered in the celebrated dome-shaped structures of ice and snow that the Europeans labeled "igloos," a generalized Eskimo word meaning "dwellings," and never killed a seal, whale, or polar bear.

But whether they lived in arctic or subarctic conditions, all Eskimos and their Aleut cousins have from ancient times shared an extraordinary ability to utilize every resource. Over the centuries, they developed a variety of sophisticated technologies and an organized system of hunting that enabled them to sustain themselves wholly on the flesh of wild animals. Their arsenal of ingenious tools included not only such weapons as the toggle-headed harpoon—carefully modified and refined to fit the particular species sought—but also remarkable modes of transportation. The seaworthy umiaks, the swift and slender one- and two-man kayaks, and sleds harnessed to teams of dogs gave hunters the means to travel vast distances across ice or water.

Eskimos everywhere were particularly resourceful in finding raw materials. The building blocks of the igloo, of course, came from the most ubiquitous materials in the Arctic—ice and snow. There were also flint and

Armed with a harpoon and a rifle, an Inupiat man prepares for a hunt in this early-20th-century photograph taken at Cape Prince of Wales, Alaska.

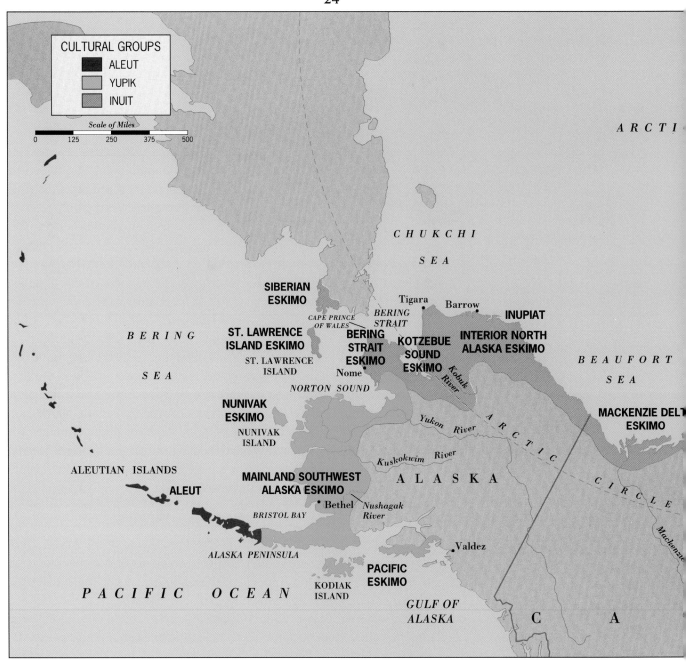

CULTURAL GROUPS
ALEUT
YUPIK
INUIT

Scale of Miles
0   125   250   375   500

A R C T I

C H U K C H I

S E A

SIBERIAN
ESKIMO

Tigara

Barrow

INUPIAT

CAPE PRINCE
OF WALES

BERING
STRAIT

B E R I N G

ST. LAWRENCE
ISLAND ESKIMO

BERING
STRAIT
ESKIMO

KOTZEBUE
SOUND
ESKIMO

INTERIOR NORTH
ALASKA ESKIMO

B E A U F O R T

ST. LAWRENCE
ISLAND

S E A

Nome

Kobuk River

S E A

NORTON SOUND

NUNIVAK
ESKIMO

Yukon River

A
R
C
T
I
C

MACKENZIE DELT
ESKIMO

NUNIVAK
ISLAND

Kuskokwim River

ALEUTIAN ISLANDS

ALEUT

MAINLAND SOUTHWEST
ALASKA ESKIMO

A L A S K A

C
I
R
C
L
E

Bethel

Nushagak
River

Mackenzie

BRISTOL BAY

ALASKA PENINSULA

Valdez

PACIFIC
OCEAN

KODIAK
ISLAND

PACIFIC
ESKIMO

GULF OF
ALASKA

C

A

other stone to be quarried for points and blades. The Avanersuarmiut, who live farther north than any other people in the world, fashioned their weapons with iron chipped from three huge meteorites. According to their belief, the meteorites represented the remains of a woman, a dog, and a tent, cast down to earth by an angry sky spirit. But the animal itself provided nearly all of the hunting gear, from shanks of bone that substituted for wood in the shaft of a lance to the double layer of caribou skin that kept the hunter comfortable in temperatures as low as -50 degrees Fahrenheit.

In addition to the tools, the Eskimos possess an amazing body of knowledge about animal behavior and climate that has been passed down over generations through oral tradition. Where the white man saw

Sprawling across much of the world's arctic region, from Siberia in the west to Greenland in the east, the Eskimos' homeland is the earth's northernmost inhabited area. Related Aleut people live in the more gentle subarctic climate of the Aleutian Islands. Geographical location and language influence what various groups are called, whether it be their own name or one given to them by post-contact Europeans. The three chief culture groups are color keyed.

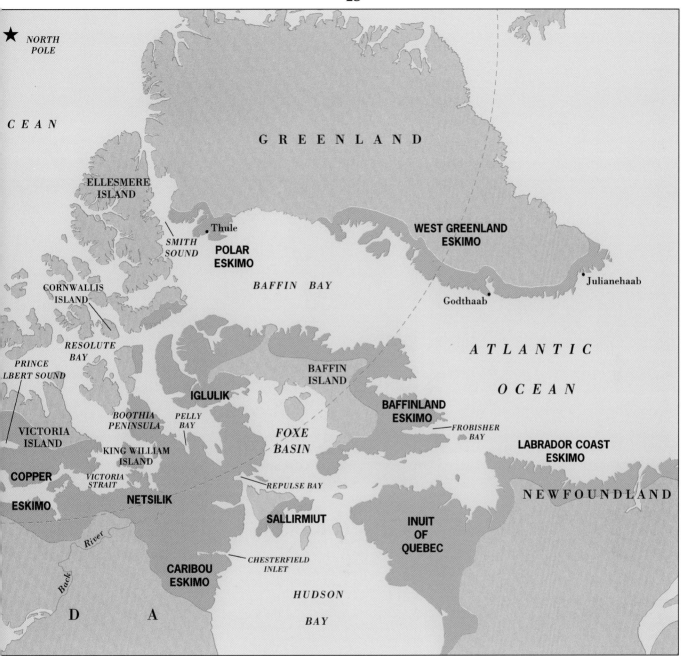

CEAN

GREENLAND

ELLESMERE
ISLAND

•Thule

SMITH
SOUND

POLAR
ESKIMO

WEST GREENLAND
ESKIMO

BAFFIN BAY

•Julianehaab

CORNWALLIS
ISLAND

Godthaab•

RESOLUTE
BAY

ATLANTIC

PRINCE
LBERT SOUND

BAFFIN
ISLAND

OCEAN

IGLULIK

BOOTHIA
PENINSULA

PELLY
BAY

BAFFINLAND
ESKIMO

—FROBISHER
BAY

VICTORIA
ISLAND

FOXE
BASIN

LABRADOR COAST
ESKIMO

KING WILLIAM
ISLAND

COPPER

VICTORIA
STRAIT

REPULSE BAY

NEWFOUNDLAND

ESKIMO

NETSILIK

River

SALLIRMIUT

INUIT
OF
QUEBEC

CHESTERFIELD
INLET

Back

CARIBOU
ESKIMO

HUDSON

D   A

BAY

only a bleak, barren desert of cold, the Eskimos saw a rich hunting ground. They knew where to find animals in trackless landscapes. They knew how to gauge wind direction and velocity with a simple staff draped with bundled shavings. They studied the sea ice ceaselessly, learning to interpret warning signs that enabled them to judge when a floe might fracture and drift away. They learned how to navigate in the thickest fog and darkest night by the feel of the ocean currents beneath their skin-covered boats. And they applied these lifesaving lessons with special qualities of temperament—courage, tenacity, self-discipline, and humor—that were just as essential to survival as know-how.

Like other original Americans, the Eskimos and Aleuts can trace their

ancestry to ancient migrations from Asia. The first wave of people passed through what is now Alaska at least 11,000 years ago. They crossed at the Bering Strait via a land bridge from Siberia created by widespread glaciation that locked up moisture from the oceans during the last Ice Age. Most of the people that Christopher Columbus subsequently dubbed Indians were descended from this first exodus. The progenitors of Eskimos and Aleuts, however, probably made the journey some 6,000 years after the first migrants—most likely by boat because by that time the land bridge had been submerged by rising seas as the massive ice sheets melted. Eskimos and Aleuts are thus biologically distinct from other Native Americans; genetically, they more closely resemble Asians.

Pinned up to dry, inflated walrus stomachs hang from a line on Saint Lawrence Island, Alaska. These stomach skins were used in the creation of musical drums.

These peoples settled along the coasts of mainland Alaska and the nearby islands, eventually diversifying in language and culture. By at least 5,000 years ago, one group occupied the Aleutian Islands off the southwest tip of the Alaska Peninsula. Relatively isolated there in friendlier temperatures, the Aleuts started evolving their own culture—separate from but similar in many respects to the Eskimo variety. Then, perhaps 3,000 years ago, Aleut diverged from the common ancestral tongue and became a separate language. At the same time, hunters of seal and caribou—forerunners of today's Eskimos—migrated from Alaska across Canada and Greenland, to sites less than 500 miles from the North Pole. The Eskimo language, having separated from Aleut, in turn branched into two tongues, Inupiaq and Yupik. The numerous dialects of Inupiaq are mutually understandable all the way from the North Slope of Alaska to the east coast of Greenland. A group of Inupiaq speakers situated in northwestern Alaska use the word for the language when referring to themselves. Inupiaq speakers in Greenland prefer to be called Greenlanders. But most who use that language call themselves Inuit, meaning "persons." They add the suffix *-miut,* meaning "people of," to the name of a geographical location when referring to a specific community (such as Tigara—Tigaramiut). Native peoples living in southwestern Alaska, south of Norton Sound, speak dialects of Yupik, a language that relates to Inupiaq much as German does to English. Ironically, the word "Eskimo" exists in neither tongue. It may have derived from a term used by Algonquian-speaking Indians of eastern Canada to mean "eater of raw meat," or it may have come from another Indian word meaning "snowshoe netter."

As the Inupiaq speakers dispersed from the Bering Strait to Greenland, a new and distinct culture evolved about AD 1000. Migrants apparently helped carry eastward these new ways, which would later be known to science as the Thule culture—named after an arctic research station and trading post in northwest Greenland established in 1910 by the part-Eskimo, part-Danish ethnographer Knud Rasmussen. From Thule, Rasmussen launched the Thule expeditions, a series of studies conducted between 1912 and 1935 that have contributed much to an understanding of the history of the Inuit. The Thule culture was marked by such key developments as the skin-covered umiaks and kayaks, dog-drawn sleds, and toggle-headed harpoons, which were established across the top of the New World by the 13th century.

The impetus for this eastward thrust may have been the bowhead whale. A climatic warming nibbled at the polar pack ice, allowing whales

Having slept through a blizzard, a sled dog emerges blanketed with snow. Protected by a double coat of fur, the dogs live outdoors year round—although during the worst weather, they are permitted to shelter in the entrance tunnel of the home.

BOON COMPANIONS

In the Far North, people have trained dogs to pull sleds for more than 4,000 years. Several Inuit creation legends link man and dog; according to one story, humans descended from a creature that was part woman and part dog. These remarkable animals, in fact, trace their ancestry directly to the wolf, and in the past, owners renewed the bloodline by staking female dogs on the tundra to crossbreed with their wild cousins. Over time, specific types of sled dog evolved, all bred for strength and endurance. During the 19th century, these legendary dogs came to be known as "huskies"—an English slang word originally applied to the Eskimos themselves.

Sled dogs are the progenitors of such popular modern breeds as the Siberian Husky, Samoyed, and Alaskan malamute. Across the Arctic, however, the people always considered them working partners, not pets. Sled dogs are still a medium of exchange, and often are given as wedding gifts. Above all, sled dogs have enabled the Eskimos to prevail in the world's harshest environment. An arctic explorer once asked an Inuit how far it was to a distant ridge. The Inuit answered: "No good dogs, long way. Good dogs, close to."

An Inuit drives his team with a whip similar to the one at left. The sealskin lash is attached to a driftwood handle and decorated with carved ivory beads. A skilled driver can flick the whip on an unruly dog's ear or rump; the mere crack of a whip will often be all that is needed to break up a dogfight.

A sled driver ties booties on one of his team to protect the pads of the dog's paws from abrasive sea ice. The dogs are particularly vulnerable during the spring, when the surface of the ice becomes rough through melting during the warm days and then refreezing at night.

A hunter tosses seal meat to his dogs. With their voracious appetites, sled dogs can gulp down more than 10 pounds of meat in a single feeding. The food is scattered to discourage the dogs from fighting over it.

Puppies nestle with their mother after feeding while on the trail. If a litter is born away from camp, the "get" (puppies) are kept warm in a sack with breathing holes and carried on the sled.

While his dogs patiently wait, a driver untangles the leads. In Greenland and Canada, where the fan hitch is commonly used, sled dogs often snarl their leads. But harnessing dogs in a fan formation lessens the risk of losing an entire team in a crevice or through thin ice.

A dog team spread out in fan formation leads a procession of sleds. After a day's work pulling up to 800 pounds for 40 miles, the dogs will be fed be

...river prepares his own meal. When traveling in rough terrain or with heavy loads, drivers will dismount and help the dogs pull.

both great and small to penetrate farther into the Beaufort Sea and adjacent Arctic waters during summer. There they fed on krill and microorganisms growing at the base of the sea ice and released by melting. Migrant hunters from Alaska apparently followed in pursuit. Whales thus became an important staple not only on the northwest coast of Alaska but also among Eskimos living along the coast of western Greenland.

Among the Tigaramiut of northwest Alaska, the search for the whale was so important that it even defined the group's social structure. The *umeliks,* or "whaleboat captains," were the wealthiest men in the village. These expert hunters had attained status through energy, skill, and force of character, acquiring large supplies of boats, whaling gear, and clothing. In a society without hereditary headmen, they were the acknowledged leaders—although their authority rarely extended beyond their own families and whaling crews. Numbering six or eight members, the crew typically consisted of brothers, sons, or other kinsmen of the umelik. Under his leadership, they formed the key economic, social, and ceremonial unit in Tigara. The umelik looked after them year round to ensure their loyalty, presenting them such prized gifts as ivory knives and sealskin boot soles, and food in times of scarcity. Every time the umelik visited his underground meat cache, he was obliged to cut off at least a small chunk for his whalers and their families, as well as for any related widows or orphans.

In preparing for the whaling season, an umelik's first ritual step was to commission a skilled craftsman to carve out of driftwood the ceremonial pot his wife would use to provide a drink of fresh water to each whale taken by his crew. When the pot was nearly completed, the umelik took it and its shavings down to the sea to be dipped in the water while he sang his sacred whaling songs. Only then would the carver do the final rendering, using an ivory tool shaped like a bowhead. A new pot was carved each whaling season; its size depended on the experience of the umelik. A whaling captain who had only recently acquired a boat and crew ordered a small one. With the passing of each successful year of whaling, the pot became progressively larger. At about the same time that the umelik commissioned the sacred pot, his wife hired a seamstress to make her a new pair of special mittens, with a ruff of wolf hair around the open fingers. As a show of respect for the whale, she would wear the mittens whenever she picked up the pot, and when the actual hunt began, she would store the left-hand mitten on her husband's whaling boat as a good luck charm.

The tradition of honoring prey reflects the special relationship all indigenous peoples have with the animal realm. Native Alaskans believe that animals are endowed with spirits and that if the community acts respectfully toward them, the animals will sacrifice their bodies to the hunters. Fresh water was always the gift offered slain sea mammals because, living in salt water, they were thought to be eternally thirsty. By contrast, when a caribou was killed, whale or seal blubber was rubbed on the dead animal's nose in the belief that, as a herbivorous land mammal, it perpetually craved fat.

Most of the prehunt rituals took place in the *karigi,* a ceremonial center and social clubhouse large enough to accommodate a half-dozen or so crews. In the 19th century, Tigara had seven karigis. Each male and female of the community belonged to one of them, although only the men and boys were allowed to occupy the building. Each year when the sun passed a certain point at the end of the peninsula, indicating the advent of fall, the karigis were opened and refurbished. The first whale-hunting feast was held soon afterward, preceded by five days and nights of competitions between selected young men from each karigi. The youths competed in various tests of strength and endurance, such as rope climbing and whipping contests that ended only when one challenger surrendered. During the entire five-day period, the participants were not allowed to eat or sleep, a test of stamina that provided conditioning for the rigors of the hunt.

At night the young men and boys gathered around their elders to hear instructive tales about the origin of the world and the history of the Tigaramiut people. Experienced hunters shared their hunting lore, gave advice on proper behavior, explained the dangers of pack ice, and described what to do if someone got lost and could not find land. Using pigment ground from a soft white stone and brushes made of bird feathers, the umeliks decorated the whale-jawbone beams of the karigi with sacred paintings of bowheads being taken. The feathers for the umelik's brushes were plucked from birds that were compatible with his personal *angoaks,* or "sacred charms," which all Tigaramiut possessed. These charms were closely linked with certain animals, such as the polar bear or loon, that could lend spiritual power to help the hunters kill their prey or save themselves in times of danger. The umeliks also brought out sacred carvings, including puppet whaling crews seated in tiny whaling boats with all their hunting gear, and human and animal figurines that represented illustrious ancestors and celebrated hunts of the past. The Tigaramiut believed that whittling animals out of wood or ivory made them more proficient hunters, and as a result, many became skillful carvers.

The whalers spent every spare moment reconditioning their hunting gear. In order not to offend the whales with shabby-looking equipment, the men cleaned their harpoons and wooden paddles. Later they would make new sealskin floats to be attached to each harpoon line. Meanwhile, their wives made them new hunting clothes with an inner layer of caribou skin and an outer layer of waterproof sealskin. The new clothes were not only deemed pleasing to the whales but also were vital for safety's sake: A frayed seam could rip open and cause a man to suffer frostbite or even to freeze to death.

In late October or early November, as the sun's lowered path across the horizon signaled the approach of the months of darkness, the karigis were closed down, and the men turned to their principal winter occupation of seal hunting in the offshore pack ice. On the occasion of the first new moon after the closing of the karigis, the wives of the umeliks dressed up in their finest clothing, raised their ceremonial pots to the moon four times, and prayed to Alignuk, the moon-man spirit, saying repeatedly, "Alignuk, drop a whale into this pot so I can kill one next season!"

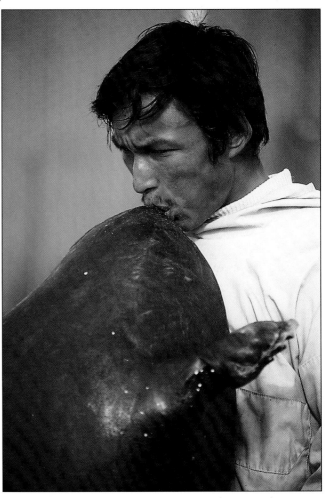

A Greenlander blows up a sealskin float in preparation for hunting on the open water. Fastened to a harpoon line, the float acts as a drag to tire wounded sea mammals when they dive and as a marker when they resurface.

The arrival of the snowbirds in late March or early April was the first sign that the bowheads were coming. Lookouts kept watch on the offshore leads—the wide, wind-driven channels that opened up in the pack ice. Typically the first whale they spotted was the beluga, a small white whale less than 15 feet long. But the beluga was a sure herald of the big black bowhead, and in the village excited children began to shout, "Puyuk-palgok!"—"They are spouting!"

At this time, the women began sewing sealskins together to make new covers for the whaling boats, or umiaks. This flat-bottomed vessel, framed with driftwood or whale bone, was about 15 to 20 feet long and up to five feet wide. It was light enough to haul over the ice and yet remarkably stable and resilient in the perilous currents around the pack ice. To ensure its safety, tradition dictated that each umiak be refitted in a special snowhouse, or *umiivik,* and only when the wind blew from the north, the "male" direction in Tigaramiut lore. Custom also called for these final days of preparation to be marked by solemnity and sexual abstinence.

The exact timing of the hunt depended on weather and ice conditions. The umeliks made the final determination, in consultation with the village

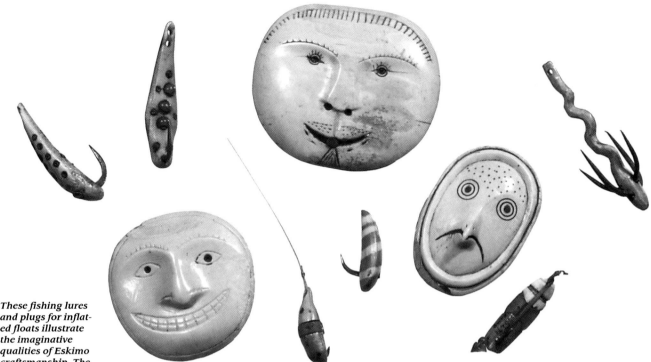

These fishing lures and plugs for inflated floats illustrate the imaginative qualities of Eskimo craftsmanship. The faces on the plugs represent male and female charm images. The lures are specialized to catch various fish, including sculpin, grayling, and herring.

elders and *angatkoks,* or "shamans." The 40 or so crews pulled their boats, laden with gear and provisions, across the ice to the open lead on sleds shod with ivory runners. Behind each crew walked the wife of an umelik, and in the rear of each procession came the umelik himself. He wore new boots on which his wife had sewn a band of white hide; every year of hunting, the width of the band increased, so that a veteran umelik might wear boots that were entirely white. As he walked, he sang his whaling songs. He and his crewmen carried in their clothing charm boxes containing tiny stone whales and other amulets to ward off danger and ensure success. Reaching the water, the group performed a final ritual. The crew paddled a short distance away and then returned to shore where the umelik's wife lay on the ice, exactly where the boat had been launched, facing inland. She remained still and quiet, mimicking the docile behavior desired of the whale. A crewman with a harpoon stood ready in the bow as if to plunge the weapon into her. But he dipped the harpoon into the water instead, and the boat turned seaward again. The wife, never looking back, returned home. There she would cease almost all normal activity, remaining tranquil so that the whale, too, would be calm and submissive.

Meanwhile, the crews spread out on the edge of the pack ice to await a sighting, one or two miles off Tigara's south shore. They might remain on the ice for as long as two weeks, returning to the village to rest only when the south wind temporarily closed the leads. It was onerous duty. Protected only by a windbreak thrown up with blocks of ice, some of the crew members slept seated on the boat sled while others kept watch. Ancient taboos forbade them the luxuries of a shelter or a fire. Only the anticipated exhilaration of the hunt eased the tedious wait.

Having tethered his dogs, a Greenlander pushes his sled over melting sea ice to join his partner at a fishing site. To avoid plunging into the frigid w

...ays close attention to the color of the puddles: Light blue indicates the underlying ice is thick enough to cross; dark blue means the ice is too thin.

When a crew spotted a whale, the men jumped into their umiak, which was kept poised over the water's edge, and paddled furiously after the quarry. Their aim was to get as close as possible to the whale during the five to 30 seconds when it surfaced to breathe. Then the harpooner in the bow could thrust his slate-tipped weapon directly downward into the animal's head, aiming for the spinal cord, with great force and a slight twisting motion. The harpoon's toggle head could rotate in the ivory socket of the slender wooden shaft on which it was mounted. When the head's sharp tip penetrated beneath skin and blubber and the animal tried to lurch away, the head remained firmly anchored while the shaft fell free. A thick rawhide line attached to the harpoon head was payed out by the crew as necessary. Two or three inflated sealskins were tied to the line to serve as floats to mark the position of the whale and help force it back to the surface when it submerged. As the hunters tried to maneuver the boat into position for the kill, the harpooner and the umelik intoned their whaling songs, first spitting into the water so that the ancient words would reach their quarry even when it dived.

Alerted by the activity, other boat crews rushed to help out. Their assistance was welcome, for although the bowhead was a relatively slow swimmer, its size made it exceedingly dangerous. If the animal surfaced underneath the umiak, it could easily capsize the vessel with one mighty shake of its enormous head or flick of its powerful tail. No one could survive more than a few minutes in these icy waters. There was also the danger that an ill-placed harpoon head might jerk free and recoil against the crew. Harpoons hurled from other boats helped stabilize the whale while hunters moved in to stab it with flint-pointed lances aimed at the heart, brain, and other vital organs. Tradition dictated that the first eight boats to arrive at the scene would be rewarded with the appropriate proportions.

These two wooden face charms were mounted inside a kayak to protect its owner from water spirits. By tradition, the smiling male image was attached on the right side of the cockpit; the frowning female was placed on the left.

When the bowhead finally succumbed, the crew that struck the first blow led the procession of umiaks back to Tigara. Nearing shore, all the crewmen joined together in the joy shout, an exultant barking sound that resembled the cry of a sea lion. Meanwhile, a messenger carrying a part of the whale's fluke and the sacred mitten went ahead to summon the wife of the umelik whose boat was credited with the capture; thus did the villagers learn of the catch. Before proceeding with the butchering—a task that might require two days of work by up to 40 men and women wielding

Their double-ended paddles at the ready, a number of Inupiat kayakers rest in a calm sea in this 1927 photograph. A hallmark of Eskimo culture, the sleek and swift kayak was used by all but a few inland groups.

long wooden shafts tipped with flint blades—the villagers formally greeted the whale. It had not actually died but had taken off the "outside parka," as the Tigaramiut poetically put it. According to their belief, the whale's soul would now find a new body to inhabit. The umelik's wife welcomed the whale into the community, where it would feed hundreds, by offering fresh water poured from the sacred pot that her husband had commissioned the previous autumn.

If the Tigaramiut were lucky, these scenes might be repeated many times until finally, as spring changed to summer, the whales appeared no more. Then a round of dancing and feasting marked the close of the whaling season and completed the ceremonial cycle that came year after year to Alaska's north coast—just as surely as did the mighty bowhead.

Although hunting still plays a major role in the lives of many Eskimos, modern life has inexorably altered the methods and equipment. The traditional ways of hunting, and the ceremonies and rituals that accompanied the hunt, have changed or have been abandoned in many places. The high-powered rifle has replaced the spear, the darting gun with its metal toggling harpoon and explosive charge has evolved from the traditional harpoon, the snowmobile has proved a practical improvement on the

Aleut fishermen join forces to catch a halibut, stabilizing their kayaks by linking paddles. One man pulls the large fish from the water while another prepares to kill it with a club similar to the one shown here, made in the form of a seal to give it special hunting powers.

dogsled, and the outboard boat has in many places taken over from the umiak and kayak. These products of modern technology have made the job of the hunter an easier one, while at the same time the availability of imported preserved foods, along with wage jobs that give purchasing power, means that hunting is no longer a matter of physical survival.

It was not many decades ago, however, that the people at the top of the world hunted in order to live, using methods that were passed down from generation to generation through the centuries. These traditional ways were as varied as the Eskimo tribes were diverse. While the Tigaramiut sought whales in small boats, for example, the Greenlanders hunted them in enormous umiaks laden with up to 50 men and women; female crew members went along to mend any tears in the skin covering. The hunters sometimes wore an insulating coverall garment of dehaired sealskins that trapped air inside and kept them afloat for hours, allowing them to jump in the water to butcher the whale, or even to risk climbing on the back of the wounded creature to make the kill. Meanwhile, in the

Aleut fishermen join forces to catch a halibut, stabilizing their kayaks by linking paddles. One man pulls the large fish from the water while another prepares to kill it with a club similar to the one shown here, made in the form of a seal to give it special hunting powers.

Gulf of Alaska at the other end of the Eskimo spectrum, Koniag Eskimos of Kodiak Island and Aleuts ventured out after whales in two-man kayaks. It was a dangerous undertaking and drownings were frequent, usually occasioned by sudden squalls that caused the hide cover of the kayaks to rip open. In foul weather, the hunters would lash two or three of the frail craft together to better ride out the storm.

The Koniags developed their own whale-hunting cult. Fierce looking, with a bone protruding through the pierced nasal septum and the ornaments known as labrets dangling from the lower lip, the hunters lived together during the summer whaling season in a secret society that others dared not approach. A kind of ancestor worship prevailed: Preserved bodies of distinguished whalers were kept in places of honor in caves that contained up to 20 corpses. The Koniags, like the Aleuts, paddled far from land in pairs of kayaks armed with spears rather than harpoons. About five feet long with a wooden shaft, the spear was fitted with a polished slate tip some 10 inches in length. The tip was smeared with poison made from the root of the monkshood plant. The hunter stationed in the kayak's forward cockpit attempted to launch the spear deep into the whale. His comrade in the rear cockpit then paddled backward, away from the turbulence stirred by the thrashing beast. The Koniags made no attempt to take the whale in tow. They paddled home and, sitting in front of their sacred cave, uttered incantations to cause the carcass of their prey to drift ashore in an accessible bay where it could be recovered and butchered.

Inuit peoples living in the Mackenzie delta region of northern Canada hunted beluga whales in large flotillas of kayaks. Although belugas seldom weigh more than half a ton, they contain a high proportion of meat and long sinews that are prized for thread in making waterproof boots. Traveling in large herds, beluga whales frequent polar waters during the summer to feed on salmon and other fish at the mouths of rivers and streams emptying into the Beaufort Sea. Because the belugas were too small to break through ice to breathe, entire herds often congregated in a narrow corridor or open lead, trapped by the moving and closing of the ice and fighting for breath with frantic hissing and blowing. With as many as 200 kayaks on the water, the Inuit formed a line with their boats on the sea side of the whales and, beating their paddles upon the water to control them, herded the terrified creatures toward the shoals. As the whales reached shallow water and floundered about, the oldest hunter present hurled his harpoon to signal the onslaught, and the slaughter began. A skilled hunter could sometimes take seven whales in a single outing. To increase the buoyancy of the dead beasts and make them easier to tow ashore, the men blew air into their lungs through a special tube inserted into the blowhole.

While the whale could bring spectacular bounty to the diet, the everyday staple for most coastal-dwelling Eskimos was the seal. From its various species, especially the most abundant, the ringed seal—which weighs up to 200 pounds and is identified by the white markings on its fur—they harvested meat, fat for oil lamps, waterproof skins for clothing and boat coverings, and translucent intestines for windowpanes. The less common bearded seal—sometimes nearly four times as large as the ringed seal—was valued for its size and thick hide that produced durable waterproof boot soles or, when cut in spirals, nearly 100 yards per animal of sturdy line for attaching to harpoons and tying down tents.

What made ringed seals so important, however, was their availability year round, even in the coldest, darkest days of winter. This seal is able to live beneath the thickest sea ice because it can open up and maintain small holes that enable it to surface every 15 or 20 minutes to breathe. The creature begins the process in the autumn by breaking through the newly formed ice with its head. As the weather gets colder and the ice thickens, the seal maintains the hole by gnawing at the opening with its teeth and scratching at the edges with its sharp claws. Even when the ice reaches a depth of six or seven feet, the seal keeps working away, creating a cylindrical passage leading upward to a tiny hole only an inch or so in diameter. A seal might carve out a cluster of a dozen holes. By locating the clusters, hunters made sure their families would not starve during the winter.

Groups of families moved out onto the sea ice to set up temporary settlements near the breathing holes. In making these hunting camps, which might consist of as many as 100 persons, the Eskimos demonstrated their skills of mobility. Each family moved its possessions to winter camp on sleds pulled by teams of dogs. In many regions, dogsleds could be used for 10 months on sea ice and for even longer on the ice along the shore.

The sled itself was a marvel of improvisation. About two feet wide and ranging from five to 15 feet in length, it was pieced together from the materials at hand. The two parallel runners might be wood or whale bone and shod with pieces of ivory or caribou antler. The Netsilik Eskimos of the Pelly Bay region of Canada fashioned runners from frozen fish wrapped in sealskin. They and other sled builders often mixed a sludge of pulverized moss and water to plaster on the runners. In the final step, the sled driver dribbled out a mouthful of water, which instantly froze on the runners, coating them with a thin veneer of ice for smoother sailing.

An Inuit fisherman adds an Arctic char to his catch. He has impaled the char on a leister, or three-pronged spear. The center prong impales the fish while the barbed side prongs prevent it from wriggling free.

The dogs, with their bushy, turned-up tails and hair nearly four inches long, were particularly well adapted to the bitter climate. Ideally a team consisted of seven or eight dogs harnessed in a fan-shaped formation that enabled each animal to pick its own trail and distribute the weight, lessening the odds of the entire team falling through thin ice. The driver controlled them with whistles and guttural signals, and a long whip of seal or walrus hide. Often, however, a family could afford to maintain only one or two of the beasts—working dogs consumed six or seven pounds of meat a day—and men and women often had to pitch in to help pull the sled. Owners sometimes outfitted their dogs with sealskin boots in the spring to protect their paws from the sharp ice crystals that formed during that season.

SEARCHING FOR THE NARWHAL

For centuries, hunters of Greenland have sought the narwhal, a relatively small arctic whale prized for its tasty flesh and the unusual spiral tusk of the male. During the Middle Ages and the Renaissance, many Europeans believed this intriguing creature was related to the mythical unicorn, and a tusk brought back by explorers fetched its weight in gold from noblemen anxious to possess its magical powers.

Each summer, narwhals return to the fjords and inlets on Greenland's northwest coast to feed and calve. Only the most skillful hunters succeed at harpooning these animals, which can attain lengths of up to 21 feet and weigh as much as 3,900 pounds. The harpoon head used by the hunter is tied to one end of a 60-foot line; at the other is a sealskin float, serving both as a marker and as a drag to tire the wounded beast. A harpooned narwhal may churn the water, capsizing kayaks, or it may sound up to 20 minutes before surfacing several hundred yards away.

Currently, local regulations limit the annual take to about 100 animals. Out of respect for tradition, Inuit hunters must first land a harpoon before dispatching a narwhal with a rifle.

A proud hunter displays his seven-foot trophy (left). The first man to sink his harpoon claims the tusk. Sought today as curios and for carving material, narwhal tusks still fetch high prices.

Greenland native Gerhard Kleist depicted this winter narwhal hunt near Godhavn in 1902. Some villagers harpoon and shoot the animals as they crowd together at breathing holes, while others haul away and butcher the carcasses.

A hunter flenses a narwhal (below). Eaten raw, the skin is rich in vitamin C. Preserved and fermented narwhal is a delicacy among native Greenlanders.

In times of famine, the dogs provided a last-ditch food supply. The dogs went first, then whatever parts of the sled that were edible.

As soon as the families reached the site of the temporary settlement, they erected snowhouses for shelter, and then the hunters set out for the breathing holes. They focused on areas of fresh flat ice since seals avoided old broken ice. After the dogs sniffed out the locations, each hunter took up his station at a single hole. To alert him to the arrival of the seal, he inserted into the hole a visual indicator—a piece of caribou leg sinew with a tuft of down that would flutter, or a thin rod of antler or bone that would bob up and down at the slightest disturbance. Then the hunter, resting his toggle-headed harpoon in a rack of two notched rods stuck in the snow, fixed his eyes on the indicator and waited—sometimes for hours.

This phase of the hunt required extraordinary patience and stamina, especially during the coldest and darkest times of the year. For two months during the winter, the sun never actually rose but remained just below the horizon, furnishing only a few hours of twilight each day. The hunter stationed himself downwind of the hole to prevent his scent from reaching the seal's sensitive nostrils. He might sit on a block of ice, or he might stand motionless on a strip of animal skin that insulated his boot-shod feet from the ice and muffled any sound they might make.

As soon as the indicator moved to show the presence of a seal, the hunter grabbed his harpoon and struck with all his strength. He twisted the shaft to detach it from the head and held fast to the line until the seal tired from struggling. The hunter then wielded an ice pick to enlarge the hole. He pulled the seal up and finished it off with a club or his fist. If the catch was the big bearded seal, however, a fierce struggle might ensue, and the hunter held on for dear life. It was considered shameful to let go. Eskimo folklore is replete with stories of unwary hunters being dragged down into the hole, disappearing into the abyss. Whatever the truth of these tales, there were always maimed hands to testify that the force at the end of the harpoon line was furious enough to rip off fingers.

The man who caught the seal cut a small incision in its abdomen and removed the liver to share with his comrades while the delicacy was still warm. He then stitched up the wound with a pin, strapped the carcass to his dogs, and hauled it back to camp. His wife gave the seal its ceremonial drink of fresh water, took care to skin and butcher it with a sharp knife—said to be less painful to its soul than a dull blade—and distributed the parts among the other families according to the prevailing custom.

The seal was so vital to most Eskimo groups that they lavished inge-

A Greenlander checks his net to see if a seal has become entangled in the mesh. Secured by stones above and below the ice, the nets are set in shallow water where the current is strong.

nuity on finding efficient ways to hunt it. Waiting all day at a breathing hole required so much time and manpower that some groups did it only in times of scarcity. Others commonly used nets. Made of rawhide, strips of seal hide, or even meshlike baleen, these nets were suspended vertically from floats of inflated bladders and anchored at the bottom by stone weights in the open water of bays and coves. The openings in the nets were just large enough to entangle the heads of swimming seals. At Barrow on Alaska's North Slope, Inupiat hunters utilized the nets in connection with breathing holes. They chipped numerous openings in the ice and maneuvered a sufficient number of large nets down through them to surround the breathing hole—a method that under the right conditions could harvest as many as 100 seals in a 24-hour period.

In late winter, the hunters focused on the newborn seals. After giving birth on the ice, females typically cared for their young in dens they had excavated under piled-up ice or snow near a breathing hole. These dens often were up to eight feet long and accommodated a half-dozen mothers and their silvery-furred pups, who lived there until old enough to swim. The hunters' dogs helped locate the dens. Their masters caved in the shelters and clubbed the pups to death or used them as decoys, relying on their cries to attract the mother.

Many Eskimos hunted seals much as they did whales, with harpoon and lance from kayak or umiak in openings in the pack ice. They capitalized on certain anomalies of seal behavior. Whereas the slightest sound or scent frightens these creatures from a breathing hole, in open water the sound and even the sight of another creature exerts a curious fascination.

Seals are attracted to noises such as scratching and pounding. The sealers carried a wooden handle with two to four seal claws attached to it, an implement called the *azigaun*. They maneuvered their craft up to the edge of the ice and, with this tool, scratched the ice in firm, slow, rhythmical strokes. Seals would swim up to investigate—and encounter the harpoon.

In late spring and summer, when the temperature rises above freezing, the gradual melting of the sea ice enlarges the breathing holes, and the seals emerge from the water for hours at a time to nap in the sun. Hunters stalked these basking seals, attempting to lull them by mimicking their behavior while creeping and crawling close enough to use the harpoon. It would have been a relatively straightforward matter if the seal simply dozed off and stayed asleep. But the ringed seal sleeps only in brief naps, often for as little as 10 seconds at a time. Then it typically raises its head to look around for signs of danger. To keep from alerting his prey, the

An Inuit hunter stealthily edges toward the breathing hole of a walrus. His knowledge of the animal's breathing habits tells him when to raise his harpoon for the kill.

A seal inua, or spirit, stares out from an ivory belt buckle made by a Yupik man. The buckle was probably worn by a hunter in order to increase his chances of success.

hunter disguised himself. He might wear pieces of white skin to blend in with the snow or even push an inflated sealskin ahead of him to deceive the animals into thinking that he was another seal. To protect himself from the cold, wet ice and facilitate his crawling, he might attach pieces of polar bear skin to his elbows and knees. Thus equipped, the hunter slid his body forward, stopping only when the seal jerked awake and looked around. To convince the seal that he was one of its own kind, the hunter might stroke the surface with his azigaun, or flap his arms like flippers and raise and lower himself in movements that mimicked those of the seal. Some hunters sang sealing songs to lull the creature back to sleep. After an hour or more of tedious maneuvering, the hunter would be soaking wet—and, if he was lucky, within striking distance. If so, he rose up and hurled his harpoon into the unsuspecting animal.

At this same time, another bulky mammal of the sea, the walrus, migrated northward and into the Eskimo larder. The walrus provided meat—aged walrus flippers were considered a delicacy—and its skin was used to form the hulls of boats. But the beast was most valued for its ivory tusks, used in weapon making and to provide shoes for sled runners.

Herds of walruses often hitched rides on chunks of melting icebergs borne by the winds and currents—and were waylaid there by hunters. Even in fog and poor visibility, the animals could be located by the sound of their distinctive bellowing. When the hunters discovered a herd asleep on the floating ice, they paddled up to a nearby floe and beached their boats on it. They bored holes through the ice and fastened their harpoon lines through the holes. Then they silently paddled this raft of ice to within striking distance of the animals and hurled their harpoons. The wounded and startled beasts instinctively rolled into the water, but the harpoon lines prevented them from escaping. During the summer, walruses frequently swam ashore, where the Eskimos surprised the unsuspecting creatures and killed them with clubs and lances.

In the water, however, hunters approached the walrus with utmost caution. The male especially was a formidable beast, frequently weighing more than a ton, with a thick skull that could thrust upward through thin ice to create a wide breathing space. Few Eskimos pursued the creature in the open water because a wounded walrus, flailing about desperately, could easily swamp an umiak or kayak or impale it with its tusks. The Iglulik of northern Canada would lash several kayaks together in order to gain stability, as in a storm, in case of an encounter with a walrus. Hunters imputed to the walrus supernatural powers, such as extraordinary intelligence, hearing, and malevolence.

The sea otter, another animal hunted by the Eskimos, was especially valued for its hide—a pelt with the densest, warmest pelage of any furbearing animal. The Aleuts specialized in hunting these relatively small creatures in the open water from their fabled kayaks. Hunters from Alaska to Greenland relied on the sleek and narrow kayak, but none of their vessels could outperform the craft—the forerunner of the modern-day kayak—that was put together by the Aleuts. The one-hatch version was about 15 feet long and less than two feet wide, constructed of a half-dozen seal or sea lion skins stretched over a framework of driftwood or whale bone. A skin covering was designed to fit over the hatch and snugly around the paddler to make the craft watertight. With his double-bladed wooden paddle, a skilled kayaker could propel his craft at speeds of up to seven miles per hour—and right the boat instantly if it accidentally flipped over.

Two hunting partners get ready to pull a dead walrus up through its breathing hole. A towline has been looped through incisions cut into the thick hide around the animal's neck.

The Aleut hunting technique, like that of the neighboring Koniags, was to surround sea otters with a flotilla of kayaks. When the creatures surfaced to breathe—females were often impeded by their young carried in their forepaws—the circle closed in and the hunters struck. The Aleuts utilized harpoon arrows and darts, which were short bone- or stone-tipped spears with detachable barbed heads, hurled from a board sling that enhanced both the thrust and accuracy of the throw.

In some Eskimo groups, it was not the whale, seal, or walrus that brought the most prestige to a hunter but mighty *nanook*—the polar bear. On King Island in the Bering Sea, for example, the taking of a polar bear was considered the greatest challenge to a hunter. Success became the occasion for the most glorious of ceremonial observances in honor of an individual hunter—the Anirsaak, or Polar Bear Dance.

Indeed, the polar bear is a hunter of such cunning and power as to inspire human admiration. Eskimo hunters may have learned some of their sealing techniques from observing the polar bear. The bear—camouflaged in its dense white coat in the snowy landscape—stalks seals sleeping on the ice. The bear even conceals its dark nose by covering it with a white paw. Bears also wait for seals at their breathing holes. These wily predators sometimes dig out the thick ice around the breathing hole—and then disguise the excavation with snow—to make sure they can smash through to the seal. By watching polar bears, Eskimo hunters may also have learned how to walk on thin ice: with legs spread as wide apart as possible and sliding their feet along quickly without stopping.

Hunters traveled by dogsled, tracking the bear by its large, distinctive prints in the snow. When the bear was in sight, the hunter cut loose his dogs, who rushed at it madly from all sides. The hunter then moved in with harpoon or lance, aiming for the vulnerable rib cage. He usually approached from the right side because polar bears were considered to be left-handed. He remained between the bear and its nearest refuge—open water—and took care to stay clear of the sweep of the beast's massive paws. If more than one hunter participated, all shared in the meat from the carcass, but the one who delivered the fatal thrust claimed at least half of the bearskin. Sometimes hunters attempted to entice the bear by leaving a trail with bits of seal. Once the animal was located, a hunter might lure it closer by lying on the ice and raising and lowering his body like a seal.

Hunting on the sea ice by sled or on foot presented an intrinsic peril beyond whatever danger the wounded prey might pose. At any time, the ice might fracture and break away from the main floe. Grinding and rumbling, it could swiftly drift away from shore, stranding the hunter on an is-land of ice. Year after year, hunters would disappear and eventually drown, freeze to death, or fall prey to polar bears. A few might survive by killing seals and improvising shelter until they found solid ice. An occasional stranded hunter from the north Alaskan coast stayed alive by crossing the ice to Siberia. To bolster this possibility, the wife of a man lost from the vil-lage of Tigara would perform a series of rituals. To keep her husband warm, she wore her parka in the house and placed in it a wrapping of wil-low bark with smoldering pieces of driftwood inside. She attempted to di-vine his fate by hanging up a pair of boots and studying the alignment of the insoles. She did not abandon hope until the following summer. The *in-yusuq,* or "personal soul," of a Tigaramiut lost on the ice always returned to his home, and if the wife saw or heard it enter the house and pass through the walls, she knew that her husband had died.

The pursuit of land mammals occurred on terrain less treacherous than the sea ice, but the hunt offered its own challenges. These an-imals ranged in size from hare and fox to brown bear and the shaggy-haired muskox. Although it travels in small herds, the muskox was taken with the help of dogs in the same manner as the polar bear. Eskimo dogs surrounded the herd, which formed its own circle of defense, with fe-males and the young in the middle. The hunters then picked apart the ring of bulls, one at a time, with their lances. Eskimos set traps for wolves and wolverines to obtain fur to trim their parkas. These animals were especial-ly valuable because their pelts so readily shed ice.

The most treasured by far of the land mammals was the caribou, the North American version of the reindeer. Migrating across the tundra in enormous herds, these barrel-chested beasts offered a cornucopia of products. From the skin, with its dense forest of hollow follicles trapping warm air for insulation, came warm and supple clothing, and from its sinews, strong and durable thread. From the massive antlers, present in both sexes, were derived weapons and implements of all kinds. From its stocky body—bulls weigh up to 400 pounds—the Eskimos dined on meat, delicious marrow from the leg bones, and something unique: Their only source of vegetal nutrition was the semidigested mosses and lichens tak-en directly from the caribou's stomach.

Except during the spring and fall migrations, caribou live in small groups of 20 or so, grazing on several hundred different species of vegeta-

Stone pillars roughly resembling humans stand against the sky in the Coronation Gulf region of the Canadian Arctic. In centuries past, Inuit hunters erected the cairns to divert herds of caribou into an ever-narrowing area where they could be killed en masse.

Caribou pass by the Kobuk River in northwestern Alaska during their fall migration (above). Cradling his rifle in a protective sheath, a hunter (left) carries the pelt of his caribou across his shoulders with the aid of a head strap.

tion growing on the tundra. Coastal Eskimos hunted them during the summer, paddling up rivers in large umiaks and taking along dogs to carry supplies. Inland Eskimos were able to hunt them year round, including the bagging of stragglers that failed to move with the herds. Hunters dug pitfalls in the snow and baited them with urine. They set snares to snag either antler or leg. They stalked individual animals or ambushed them from behind rocks. The usual weapon was the bone- or ivory-tipped arrow shot from close range with a bow made of wood or spliced sections of antler reinforced with sinew and strung with the skin of caribou or seal.

The hunter attempted to approach his prey undetected. He moved from downwind, first testing the wind by floating on the air a few hairs pulled from his mitten. He sought cover behind a rock or pile of ice, lying concealed for hours until the caribou came near. If the terrain offered no cover, he might imitate his quarry by pulling his parka hood over his head, stooping forward to mimic the animal's gait, and holding aloft his walking stick and bow to resemble antlers. He might even pretend to graze, wandering to and fro until the caribou came near out of curiosity or until he could approach within range. Then he pulled down the bow, dropped to one knee, and launched his arrow.

The great mass of caribou taken by inland hunters came during the communal hunts. These cooperative endeavors usually occurred twice a year when the herds numbered in the thousands—during the spring when the animals migrated north and during the fall when they returned south. Most drives focused on the fall, when the caribou wore thick summer fat and their new hair was still short and well suited for clothing. Small groups of extended families gathered from far and wide at a traditional location. Like the whale hunts of their coastal cousins, these large-scale drives served as social and ceremonial centerpieces as well as the keystone of the economy. Each band of hunters had a shaman who sang songs to call the caribou, and a leader who, with his organizational abilities and hunting skills, corresponded to the umelik of the whaling coast. Like the whalers for whom the karigi was the center of all ceremonial preparation, the inlanders built a temporary house for the observance of rituals, including a four-day period of sexual abstinence preceding the hunt.

The key feature of the typical communal drive was an elaborate trap that could funnel large numbers of caribou to their deaths. Built astride a main migratory route, it consisted of converging lines of scarecrowlike figures. These figures, intended to frighten the caribou in the desired direction, were fashioned of stone cairns topped with chunks of turf and

perhaps draped with old clothing to look like people. They were erected at intervals of 30 to 100 yards and sometimes extended as far as five miles from the intended killing ground. To make certain the caribou stayed within the funnel and moved rapidly, a yelling horde of beaters—usually women and children—chased the herd from behind.

The manner of the actual kill varied. In what was probably the oldest method—much as early Plains Indians killed buffalo—the converging cairns led to a cliff over which the rushing animals fell to their deaths. Men armed with spears dispatched any caribou that survived the plunge over

Perched on a nesting cliff, a Polar Eskimo swoops his net at a flock of auks, one of many species of migratory seabirds that return to the Arctic each spring to breed. After netting an auk, the hunter will kill it by pressing his thumb on its heart. Auks are eaten raw, boiled, or stuffed in a seal carcass to ferment into a delicacy called "giviak."

the precipice. More commonly, the herd was funneled into a corral enclosed with sod and rocks or walls of ice and snow. Some animals were caught in snares; the rest milled in confusion while hunters sprang from their blinds. Boys participating in their first caribou drive were given the privilege of firing the first arrows before the men began the destruction of the trapped herd. Sometimes the rows of cairns converged on a lake. The caribou plunged into the water and were met by hunters waiting for them in kayaks. Paddling faster than their prey could swim, the kayakers attacked with lances. The caribou that tried to escape to shore encountered ranks of women and children who scared the animals back into the depths with their shrieks and howls. Each hunter collected the animals he had killed, tied them together by their antlers, and dragged them to shore.

By any of these methods, scores of caribou could be taken on a single day—and more the next day if the migrating herd was large enough. The carcasses were butchered on the spot and divided among the hunters and others by tradition. For some groups, however, the heads had to be cut off first and placed in a separate pile in the belief this would prevent further suffering by the caribou's soul. Much of the meat was placed inside containers made from beluga whale stomachs or sealskins and cached under stones or in a pit for later use. Prime parts, including marrow from the leg bones and the green contents of the stomach, were consumed in the ceremonial feasting that followed the hunt. People gorged and played games but were careful to pay attention to sacred rituals so that the caribou would return again next season.

The same resourcefulness that characterized hunting went into the quest for fish. In most regions, fish supplemented the diet of meat, but for Eskimos living along three major rivers on the Alaska Peninsula, where five different species of salmon spawned, fish was a year-round staple. Some fishermen worked the open sea, snagging halibut, which could weigh as much as 600 pounds, on wooden hooks at the end of 900-foot-long lines fashioned from seaweeds. Most Eskimo fishing, however, took place on waters immediately offshore and on inland lakes and streams. Whitefish were caught with nets made of baleen, tomcod with ivory lures on sinew lines attached to antler poles. Lake trout were speared with a bone- or antler-tipped device, which impaled the trout with its central prong and grasped it firmly between the two flexible outer prongs.

Fishing in winter required enormous effort and endurance. Among the Copper Eskimos, for example, a fisherman used a chisel of ivory or antler to painstakingly chip a hole about a foot in diameter through five or six feet of ice, pausing every minute or two to scoop out the pieces. He then dropped in his line with its barbless hook of bone or antler attached to a fish-shaped decoy and sat or knelt in the cold on a mat of caribou skin. All the while he jigged his line, jerking it up and down so that the rhythmic motion of the lure would attract a lake trout or other fish close enough to be hooked. During the course of a day's work, an Eskimo angler might chisel out as many as four or five different holes.

These sparse results contrasted sharply with the bountiful harvests of migratory fish. In the late summer, when masses of salmon swam upriver to spawn in tributary streams, they frequently encountered barriers erected by the Eskimos. These barriers might be simply an angled wall of piled-up stones that funneled the fish into a kind of underwater corral, where they could be dispatched by spear. More elaborate was the semipermanent weir consisting of posts supporting a screen of lashed-together spruce splints and roots interspersed with cone-shaped traps, from which hundreds of salmon sometimes were collected in a few hours.

For the Eskimos who lived along Alaska's Kobuk River, salmon harvests represented one of the rare instances in which women performed the vital task of food procurement in addition to their regular duties. Women took complete charge of fishing in late summer while the men went off to the mountains to hunt caribou. Their implements, seines made from the inner bark of willow trees, were kept folded and ready in large bark canoes. When lookouts downstream sighted the rippling water signaling the ascent of the salmon, pairs of women dashed to each canoe. One grabbed an end of the seine and stayed ashore while the other woman paddled out to pay out the net. As the salmon became ensnared, she paddled back toward shore, where the children helped haul in the teeming net, stilling the larger fish with wooden clubs.

So enormous was the need for meat—an adult Eskimo might consume up to eight pounds per day—that no source was overlooked, including birds. Of the score of species of migratory birds that nested in the arctic regions every summer, the favorite ones hunted for food were ducks, geese, and the ptarmigan, a tasty partridgelike bird that offered the additional attraction of flying in large flocks low to the ground. The Aleuts and Koniags fashioned warm, frocklike parkas from the skins of the cormorant and puffin. The feathers and feet were appropriated for ornamentation and ceremonial objects.

Birds were taken by a variety of means. They were snared, netted, shot

A band of Siberian Chukchi duck hunters wear bolas wrapped around their heads similar to the one at left, made of ivory weights and sinew. The whirling bolas brought down birds on the wing; when hunting over water, Eskimos used bola weights made of buoyant driftwood.

with bow and arrow and multipronged darts flung from a throwing stick, and lured into stone enclosures with decoys. They were also plucked from the air by the bola, a device in which a half-dozen or so oval weights of ivory or bone were attached to lengths of braided sinew. These cords, about 30 inches long, were bound together by bird quills in a kind of handle. Grasping this, the hunter whirled the bola around his head once or twice and then flung it at a low-flying flock. Wheeling through the air, the weights of the bola could wrap around a bird at an effective range of up to 40 yards and force it helplessly to earth. During migration season, some hunters carried a bola with them in a pouch slung around the neck to be ready at an instant's notice in case a flock of waterfowl flew by.

The taking of birds was customarily the first step employed in the training of the neophyte hunter. At a very early age, a boy learned to shoot arrows at ducks from a miniature bow and to lie patiently in the cold holding the end of a rawhide thong until a gull stepped into the baited snare. A boy's coming of age in western Greenland typified the apprenticeship. When he was 10 years old, he was given his first kayak so that he could hunt birds and fish with his peers; at age 15, he began hunting caribou, seals, or even whales with his father. His first major kill occasioned a feast at which he was called upon to describe the hunt in loving detail. Guests in turn praised his skill and commented on the excellent quality of the meat. His people had gained another hunter, elevating the odds for survival in the ceaseless struggle with ice and snow. ◆

PURSUING THE GREAT NANOOK

Near the end of a short spring day, Eskimos with sled dogs specially trained to track polar bears head for traditional hunting grounds off northwest Greenland.

For at least 1,000 years, the frozen wastes of Melville Bay along the northwest coast of Greenland have been the setting for a grueling odyssey. Every spring Polar Eskimo hunters hitch up their sled dogs and set off on a perilous quest that will last a month or more. They endure sub-zero cold, gale-force winds, and treacherous ice that piles 15 feet high to block their path and threatens to fracture into floes that will strand them. The purpose of this annual ordeal is to track down and kill the magnificent creature known as nanook—the polar bear.

Huge, wily, and dangerously unpredictable, the polar bear is the Eskimos' most formidable quarry. The full-

grown male typically weighs between 900 and 1,600 pounds, and the female about half that amount. Ungainly in appearance, with elongated bodies, narrow heads, and long necks, these animals nevertheless move with grace and swift agility. Loners by nature, they seek the company of others only during the mating season, and then they separate.

Polar bears prowl the frozen sea just offshore during the spring to prey on seals and fish. They wait patiently for seals to rise to the top of their breathing holes; then they make the kill by smashing their prey with a powerful swipe of the paw. They stalk humans only when starving—but fight to the death when confronted by the hunter and his huskies.

Even with the advantage of modern firearms, Eskimos consider the polar bear such a daunting challenge that only the most skilled hunters and dogs are chosen for the chase. They prize the flavor of the bear's flesh and the warmth of sleeping pads and water-resistant trousers fashioned from its luxurious pelt. But above all, traditional Polar Eskimo culture values the hunt as the supreme test of a young man's mettle. In that area of Greenland, a suitor is not deemed worthy of the daughter of a great hunter until he has taken his first nanook.

Stopping for the night, the hunter shown in the photographs at left wraps himself in a polar bear skin to remind his huskies of the creature that they have been trained to sniff out, harass, and surround. In order to work them into a frenzy and heighten their ardor for the chase, he puts on the head, growls, and feigns a polar bear attack (lower left).

Improvised shelter, heated and illuminated by the fire of a portable kerosene stove, furnishes overnight protection against the wind and cold on Melville Bay. Inside the shelter, a pair of sleds that have been overturned side by side form a platform for sleeping. Harpoon shafts stuck in the ice serve as tent poles to support the canvas covering.

Below, paw prints in the snow covering the sea ice provide clues that enable the experienced hunter to estimate the quarry's size and rate of travel. He also can tell how recently the bear made the print: The harder the ridge of snow between the sole pad and the toe depressions, the older the tracks. Here, the soft snow signifies a fresh trail perhaps only minutes old. At right, hoping to glimpse the bear, the hunter perches on an icy pinnacle and, keeping his eager dogs in hand, scans the horizon. After sighting the bear, hunters usually jettison nonessential supplies to lighten their sleds for the chase. To avoid spooking their quarry, they pursue the bear in silence, communicating through sign language or occasional bird calls.

Harassed by a snarling husky, the doomed bear struggles to break free from the harpoon line anchored in its flank. The drama began when hunters unleashed their dogs to corner the animal, and the first man within rifle range took aim and fired, hitting the prey in the foreleg. The wounded bear scrambled into the water, but the harpoon stopped it from swimming away. Game until the end, the beast seized the line between its paws and tried to bite through it. A rifle shot to the head finished the bear off.

With the harpoon line looped around the dead bear's neck, successful hunters strain to haul the 1,000-pound carcass onto firm ice. Although the hunt remains difficult and dangerous work, modern firearms lessen the peril. Before high-powered rifles made it possible to work from a safe distance, hunters had to move in close, thrusting with lances that the enraged bear sometimes seized and snapped off like toothpicks.

Moving quickly before the carcass freezes, the hunter above starts to strip away the bear's skin with his knife. At right, he stretches out the bloodstained pelt to divide it up. By custom, the skin was measured out with the shaft of a harpoon. The top half, as well as the best cuts of meat, was awarded to the hunter who struck the first blow; the remainder went to the other men. To celebrate the kill, they ate boiled bear meat, sharing their repast with the dogs but avoiding the liver, which contains poisonous concentrations of vitamin A. Upon returning to the village, each man would have his share of the skin made into a pair of trousers that would symbolize his proud achievement and keep him warm on the next hunt.

THE GIFT OF THE WHALE

During the time that photographer Bill Hess recorded these Inupiat whale hunts off northwestern Alaska in the 1980s, he sensed a primeval spiritual connection between hunter and hunted. "The whale appeared to bow," he marveled on one occasion, "as if, in spirit, it knew the hunters were waiting for it."

Just as sled dogs have been replaced by gasoline-powered snowmobiles over the years, ancient taboos

banning shelter and fire from the whale hunters' camps have yielded to the comforts of insulated tents and modern camp stoves. Yet strong vestiges remain of traditional ceremonies of reverence. Cleanliness, for example, is an essential demonstration of respect for the spirit of the whale. When Hess carelessly put a pot down in the wrong place, a captain barked, "Whales do not give themselves to crews who keep sloppy camps!"

The killing of the whale is no less reverent because it is aided by explosive harpoons. The rites of thanksgiving may be casual, truncated, and expressed in Christian terms nowadays, but they remain an important connection between the spirit of the Inupiat and the spirit of the whale. "We have been living on the ice for thousands of years," one captain explained to Hess. "We have developed a kindred relationship with this great animal."

The captain of a whaling crew shouts in triumph (above) as he sees the whale he has harpooned rise to the surface, motionless—a clean kill. Men using a block and tackle (left) winch a 50-ton bowhead onto the ice for butchering. The women who will assist have observed tradition by waiting at a distance for word of success.

DANCING FOR THE SPIRIT OF THE BEAST

After more formal rituals of thanksgiving have been performed, youngsters mount the leviathan's carcass to perform dances and songs.

REMOVING THE WHALE'S "PARKA"

Holding his flensing knife, a captain prepares to strip the whale's skin and blubber—to the Inupiat, the "outside parka" of the whale's immortal spirit. The first section, cut out before the whale was beached, is already being boiled to provide snacks.

Women of the community distribute steaming morsels of boiled blubber (below, top) to sustain the workers. An elder (with head upraised, bottom) offers a prayer of thanksgiving and asks for continued blessings on the people and the whales. Although the prayer is Christian, it follows closely the ancient forms of obeisance to the spirit of the whale.

SHARING THE LEVIATHAN'S BOUNTY

Workers divide the massive chunks of blubber and meat into shares for distribution to members of the hunting and butchering crews. There will be plenty for everyone, and the remainder will be stored in the permafrost to supply the community's annual feasts until the onset of the next whaling season.

With the carcass almost picked clean, women glean the last pieces of the meat for making a delicacy called "mikigaq"—fermented whale meat.

THE FEAST OF THANKSGIVING

Community members pray before the feast that ends the whaling season—a celebration held, said one, "to let the whale know we are happy."

2

"NEVER WEARY OF LAUGHTER"

Members of an Inuit family sit with their dog outside their temporary summer dwelling, a tent, or "tupik," made of animal skins strung on poles and anchored by rocks against the Arctic's bitter winds. From the tent hang inflated sealskins used for food storage.

In September of 1938, Jean-Pierre Gontran de Montaigne de Poncins arrived at King William Island in the central Canadian Arctic to fulfill a quixotic dream. A restless and troubled man, the 38-year-old French aristocrat yearned to experience the "simplicity and directness" of Eskimo life. For the next nine months, he did just that, traveling by dogsled across thousands of miles of ice-covered ocean and tundra, sleeping in temporary igloos at night, and enduring temperatures that plunged as low as -50 degrees Fahrenheit for days on end with the Netsilik Eskimos, or as they call themselves, the Netsilingmiut, "people of the ringed seal."

As their name implies, the Netsilik were primarily hunters of seal—although they also depended heavily on the migrating herds of caribou that passed through their vast 50,000-square-mile domain each summer and fall as well as on the Arctic char that abounded in the region's countless lakes and rivers. Numbering probably no more than 500 persons at the time of Poncins's visit and divided into several bands of self-sufficient families, these hardy nomads had been almost entirely cut off from the outside world until the late 19th century when they began trading for guns and steel tools with whaling fleets at Chesterfield Inlet and Repulse Bay on the northwest coast of Hudson Bay. In 1938, however, many of them still lived in the traditional manner.

Poncins was ill suited for Eskimo life. Beyond a few tins of biscuits, tobacco, and tea, he had little to contribute. He could not spear a fish through a chiseled hole in the ice or spot a seal two miles away. He hated to beat dogs, a customary method of discipline. He knew nothing of tying useful knots, or of processing hides, or of differentiating between types of snow. His fingers and toes, unaccustomed to the cold, were easily frostbitten, forcing him to spend many days inside his hosts' igloos, painfully recuperating. But the Netsilik accepted this rare kabloona—their word for "white man"—and tolerated his strange and amusing ways.

Gradually Poncins adapted to the rigors of Eskimo life, and he began

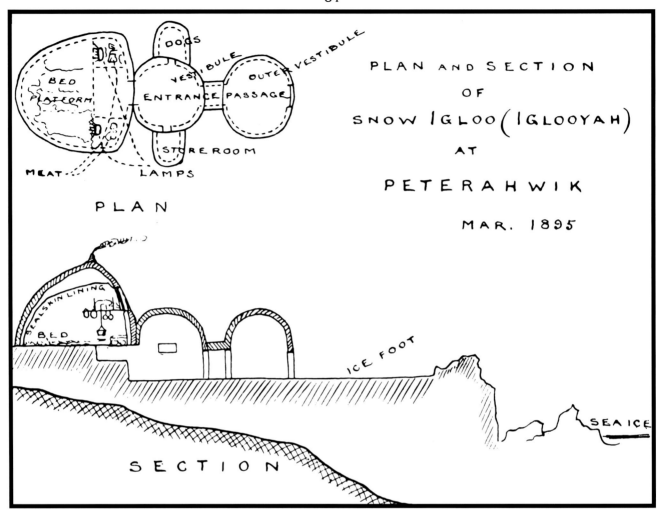

PLAN AND SECTION OF SNOW IGLOO (IGLOOYAH) AT PETERAHWIK MAR. 1895

DOGS

VESTIBULE

OUTER PASSAGE

VESTIBULE

BED PLATFORM

ENTRANCE

STOREROOM

MEAT

LAMPS

PLAN

SEALSKIN LINING

BED

ICE FOOT

SEA ICE

SECTION

to appreciate his hosts. He marveled at their uncanny ability to turn a few raw materials—snow and ice, skin, bone, and stone—into lifesaving implements. He admired their physical strength and their matchless hunting and fishing skills, their respect for individual liberty, and their stoicism and unflinching courage in the face of adversity.

Poncins came to realize that every aspect of Eskimo life—from the aptness of their technology to the way they thought and acted—had evolved in response to the harsh conditions under which they had lived so long and successfully. Even their physical nature—medium height, with relatively long torsos and short legs, powerful jaws and teeth, fewer sweat glands overall and highly concentrated in the face, thick black hair, and high basal metabolism—seemed tailored to support survival in the unforgiving climate. The Frenchman began to relish the Netsilik diet of raw fish and boiled seal meat and blubber, discovering that the fat and protein greatly enhanced his ability to withstand the cold. (Although Poncins did not know it at the time, seal liver also contains high concentrations of vitamin C.) Their good humor further invigorated him. "These Eskimos afforded me decisive proof that happiness is a disposition of the spirit," he observed. "They were a cheerful people, never weary of laughter."

The drawing above shows top and side views of an igloo that Admiral Robert Peary observed at Peterahwik in Greenland during his 1895 expedition to map the polar icecap. Made by a member of the expedition, the sketch shows a double-vestibule entry with side storerooms for food and gear.

But most of all, Poncins valued their communal spirit. The Netsilik seemed to share everything, as long as it lasted, and the sense of acceptance that Poncins felt when he lived among them was like nothing he had ever experienced before. "Those men about whom I knew properly nothing at all had stood shoulder to shoulder with me in the blizzard," he wrote movingly. "Day after day, a wind would rise, a sign of danger would appear in the air, and we would respond together, each forgetting himself, and striving in the common cause. Outside, it wanted war and flood to give man this sense of brotherhood; here it was a commonplace of life."

As he learned more about Netsilik ways, Poncins came to realize that the friendliness extended to him, a European, was traditionally reserved for kinspeople and the network of relations that an individual Eskimo might develop in the course of a lifetime. The strong sense of group solidarity that Poncins so admired prompted most Eskimo peoples, including the Netsilik, to treat strangers of their own race with suspicion and hostility. Indeed, in certain instances in early times, a lone Eskimo who entered the camp or village of non-kin risked being killed.

Near the end of his arctic adventure, Poncins trekked to Pelly Bay, at that time a remote settlement located several hundred miles from the nearest trading post. Indeed only a handful of outsiders, primarily missionaries and traders, had ever ventured into the area. But the Netsiliks who wintered there welcomed him into their homes. "The generosity and courtesy of their hospitality struck me as forcibly as the grace of their life," Poncins later wrote. "Hardly had I come into the igloo before my clothes were taken from me, my boots and socks drawn off my feet and hung to dry on the rack. It was as if my presence honored the igloo, and when my clothes were later handed back to me by a little girl in a gesture whose shyness was charming, I saw that they had not been dried only, but scraped clean and soft as well."

Fringe-decorated leather briefs like those below from Alaska's Saint Lawrence Island were sometimes the only garment worn by both men and women when inside their igloos and sod houses where, as one observer reported, the air often became tropically hot.

Poncins had observed a tiny slice of a truly remarkable phase of human history. Within a few years, military airstrips, radar stations, and supply depots would be constructed at Pelly Bay. Like other arctic and subarctic peoples before them, the Netsilik would be compelled to abandon a way of life that had served them well for centuries and conform to the exigencies of the modern industrialized world. Much is known about that traditional life, in large part because it persisted in isolated areas, such as Pelly Bay, for such a long time—and because the various Eskimo peoples have worked so hard to preserve their rich and complex heritage in the face of wrenching cultural transition.

The ingenuity and practicality of the people of the ice and snow are perhaps nowhere more clearly evidenced than in their traditional clothing, sewn by the women out of carefully tanned animal skins, with bone or ivory needles and thread of twisted beluga or caribou sinew. Eskimo men and women typically wore suits of caribou skin of varying lengths and designs, although the fur of other animals might be substituted, depending on the region. In winter, they normally wore two sets, an inner garment with the fur turned against the body and an outer parka with the fur turned to the air. The best skins for clothing came from caribou taken in the fall when the animal was in the process of growing its dense coat for the coming winter. Except in the Pacific region, most Eskimo parkas had hoods, with ruffs of wolf or wolverine fur to protect the face. A tight-fitting bird-skin undershirt with the feathers against the skin might also be worn. Water-resistant mittens and boots made of sealskin or caribou skin protected the hands and feet. Dried grass, down, or moss was sometimes placed inside the boots and mittens for insulation and the absorption of moisture. Sometimes rabbit-skin stockings and loose bearskin trousers were also worn. In summer, Eskimos generally wore garments made of lighter skins, such as seal, or simply stripped down to their winter inner garments, with the fur turned out instead of in.

Traditional Eskimo architecture was as well conceived as their clothing. During the short summer months, the season of intensive gathering of stores for the bleak winter ahead, most Eskimo groups lived in animal-skin tents propped up by poles of driftwood or willow. With the coming of winter, however, they settled down at campsites or villages and moved into their permanent homes to make new clothing, weapons, and other goods from the bundles of raw materials collected over the summer.

Eskimo winter homes shared many common features. Most were domelike, semisubterranean structures, dug into hillsides, with a low entrance tunnel that kept the icy winds from blowing into the house, and usually had to be traversed on hands and knees. At the end of this passageway was a door covered with skins to further keep out the draft. A platform or bench lined the walls of the main room for sleeping or sitting. A small ceiling hole, the "nostril" of the house, provided ventilation, while a skylight or window with a pane of clear ice or scraped seal or walrus gut

SNUG HOUSES FOR THE LONG WINTERS

Proof of the Eskimos' ability to cope with their harsh environment were the cozy permanent homes, pictured here and on the next pages, that they began building centuries ago for shelter during the fierce winter months. Called sod houses, the dwellings were engineered to withstand the killing cold and murderous winds of the worst arctic storms, remaining so snug that Eskimo men and women were able to go about their indoor tasks half-clothed, warmed solely by their own body heat and the flames from oil lamps.

Key to this comfort was insulation provided by the earth itself. Eskimo builders first dug down about three feet to hollow out a main living space. Over it they erected a frame made of whatever the barren region provided, usually driftwood or whale bones. On the framework they piled layers of sod and other materials. Making the houses even snugger were sunken entrance tunnels that permitted fresh air to seep in but kept cold winds out. Enlarging the design, the Eskimos also built communal sod houses big enough to hold the people of an entire village for dances and other rituals.

Eskimos occupied their houses most of the year. They left them in winter only for hunting trips, and in the summer when the ground began to melt, they moved into tents. So well suited were sod houses for life in the Arctic that Eskimos all across the great frigid reach from Alaska to Greenland built similar dwellings, giving them up only in this century for more modern structures.

Neatly tucked into a dune, an empty sod house stands amid blowing sea grass in an abandoned village at Yukok on the Alaskan coast of the Bering Sea.

INSIDE THE EARTHEN DOMES

The simple but efficient designs of a north Alaskan coastal communal sod house, called a *qargi* by the Inupiat, and a smaller family dwelling are shown in the cutaway drawing below. Beneath its domed roof covered with layers of sod, stones, and sometimes insulating animal skins, a family home consisted mainly of a single room about 15 feet across and eight feet high that could accommodate from eight to 12 relatives of several generations. Virtually the only furniture was a raised platform, where the house's owner and honored relatives ate and slept, the rest of the family using the planked floor. In the entrance

tunnel, the Eskimos hollowed out al-
coves for storing clothes, hunting gear,
and food, and a space where the
women of the family did the cooking.
    The large communal houses were
similar in structure, with sleeping plat-
forms and entrance tunnels leading to
holes in the floor. Like family houses,

qargis often had ventilation holes in
their roofs to let fumes from oil lamps
escape, and ingenious windows made
of translucent seal intestine that let in
light during the day and, when lighted
at night from the inside by whale-oil
lamps, acted as beacons for hunters
coming home in the winter darkness.

*Striking a drum while he sings, an Inupiat
man entertains his fellow villagers who
lounge on the sleeping platform and against
the walls of the communal sod house, pictured above, that sits in the center of a village of other moundlike houses. At left, a
woman prepares a meal in the cooking
space of the tunnel of her house while another sews in the living chamber above.*

A vital tool in all Eskimo homes was a snow-beater, often made of bone like the one at left, that was used to knock snow off clothes before it melted and soaked the fur.

let in a little bit of light. Side chambers provided extra space for storage and cooking, and there might also be a meat cache dug into the permafrost. Each home also contained a wooden bucket for storing the family's urine for use in treating wounds and processing hides. Although the Kodiak Islanders and many Yupik groups inhabited multifamily houses, most Eskimos lived in single-family dwellings. Nevertheless, it was not unusual for them to share a winter house or a summer tent with one or more extended-family members—a widowed father, perhaps, or a brother and his wife. Related families frequently built their houses side by side with a common entrance tunnel.

Building materials varied, depending on the region. Most homes were constructed of sod, stone, and driftwood—although maritime peoples, such as the Nunivak Islanders in the Bering Sea and the North Alaska Inupiat, also used bowhead whale bones and skulls for beams and other kinds of supports. Some Yupiks living below the timberline in southern Alaska built houses out of logs, chinked with mud, like their Athapaskan-speaking Indian neighbors. Even though almost every Eskimo group knew how to make the celebrated snow igloo as a temporary shelter while traveling, generally it was the Eskimos who hunted in the vast area extending from the Canadian Arctic eastward to northern Greenland who actually lived all winter in them.

The responsibility for carving the igloo normally fell to the man of the family. It required a sophisticated knowledge of snow. After carefully selecting the site according to the snow's consistency—it must be firm, at least a foot deep, and not granular—he cut out blocks of snow with his snow knife, a tool often made out of ivory or antler and shaped like a broad-bladed saw. His wife and children worked alongside him, filling in any holes or cracks in the outer walls with snow.

To watch an Eskimo build an igloo was to see a true artisan at work. The Frenchman Poncins recalled observing his guide erect an igloo after a long and tiring trek across the tundra: "Choosing his snow, he moved like a man inspired, bowed over, digging in his harpoon first here, then there, moving at first swiftly, then slowly, prodding the snow with a gentleness as if afraid to hurt it. Carefully, he cut out a first row of blocks and fitted them in a circle round him. Now he stood within them, not to emerge again until his work was done. The blocks for the higher rows would be cut out from beneath his feet, and he knew to a square foot what lay where he stood. Slowly, cautiously, he built up the gradual spiral that was to be his house. Bent far over, only his rounded back showing above the first row of blocks, he dealt fine precise blows with his snow knife. He hoisted a block, its inner surface cut on the appropriate bias, and trimmed with light strokes until the block slipped into its place."

After the shell was completed, the guide's wife crawled inside and prepared the interior of the dwelling, piling up a bank of snow to make a table that also served as a sleeping platform. The woman then covered the platform with mats of willow twigs and animal-skin bedding and unpacked the family's other belongings. Depending on how long the family intended to stay, she might also line the wall with animal skins—usually the same ones that were used for the family's summer tent. To warm the igloo, she pounded a chunk of frozen blubber until it released oil and then placed the dripping piece in a lamp.

Like the snow igloo, Eskimo lamps were marvels of simplicity. Most of them consisted of a small oval of hollowed-out soapstone with a wick fashioned from a piece of moss or heather. The wick was cut into a sawtooth pattern and placed on the rim of the lamp, partially floating in the melted blubber. Frequently the lamp was set on a tripod of stones at an angle in order to regulate the flow of oil to the wick—an art all Eskimo women mastered. In a well-made igloo, a single seal-oil lamp radiated enough heat to allow the occupants to strip to the waist. As the temperature rose, the igloo's ceiling would begin to drip. To avoid a steady trickle

The carved head and torso of a woman emerge from the bowl of a soapstone lamp from Alaska's Kenai Peninsula. Traditionally essential in all Eskimo homes, oil lamps burned blubber from seals or whales, which fed wicks of moss laid in the grooves cut in the lamp's rim.

SHELTERS MADE OF SNOW

The snow structures called igloos, which served as temporary shelters during winter hunting trips, required experience and skill on the part of the builder. First a hunter had to find an area covered with exactly the right sort of hard-packed snow. Next, standing inside a circular outline of the planned shelter, he sliced the snow into blocks of graded sizes, large ones for the foundation layer, thinner ones for the upper walls. The blocks cut, he beveled the top edge of each slightly before fitting them together so that the walls would slant inward, converging to form a dome.

All this had to be done with great speed—often in the winter dark—to escape the killing cold. An experienced hunter could make an igloo in less than three hours working alone, although usually another hunter or the man's wife pitched in to help.

The result of this furious but precise labor was a compact, warm, and windproof shelter. Nowadays few Eskimo peoples use igloos—hunters mostly employ tents—but a number of expert builders remain, such as the Greenlander named Qaviganquag, seen on these pages. In addition, many communities continue to hold igloo-making contests to keep the ancient skill alive.

Working skillfully with a small saw, Qaviganquag slices slabs of snow for an igloo's walls from the area that, once hollowed out, will serve as its floor. Traditionally, hunters employed special knives to cut the snow, such as the 14-inch-long, 19th-century ivory blade from Alaska shown below. The knobs on the handle, shaped like seal heads, provided the workman a secure grip.

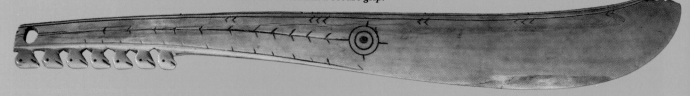

Working inside his foundation walls (left), Qaviganquag trims the tops of the blocks so the next layer will fit exactly and tip inward at the correct angle. Then he deftly twists a capstone block (lower left) into its hole on the top of the dome. Next he will plaster all the cracks with loose snow to make the structure weather-tight. At bottom, Qaviganquag relax-es inside the igloo on a sleeping plat-form of snow left in-tact during con-struction. His body heat and the kerosene lamp will warm the igloo.

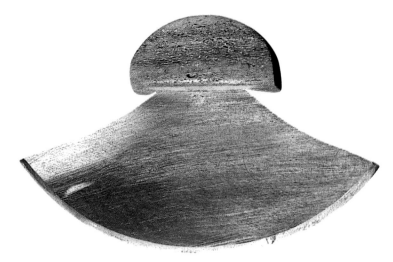

The compact knife, or ulu (left), fashioned of a rounded blade attached to a wood or bone handle was used by Eskimo women for everything from skinning animals to chopping ice.

of ice water, the occupants constantly scraped away the melting snow to expose colder layers underneath.

The availability of blubber from seals, whales, and other sea mammals made a substantial impact on the Eskimo standard of living. By burning oil from blubber, the *tagiugmiut,* or "sea people," could maintain comfortable temperatures as high as 90 degrees Fahrenheit in their winter houses. In contrast, the materially poorer *nunamiut,* or "land people," suffered during the cold weather. Among such groups were the Caribou Eskimos, who hunted and fished on the tundra between Back River and Chesterfield Inlet northwest of Hudson Bay. These people had to use inferior fuels such as caribou tallow, marrow, and fish oil in their lamps, and the temperature inside their homes rarely rose above freezing in the winter. For cooking, Caribou Eskimo women gathered bundles of dwarf birch, heather, willow, and other tundra plants. Harvesting the plants was a grueling task, especially in the winter when the women had to scrape away the snow and pull out the roots from the frozen ground with their bare hands. After a few years of this labor in sub-zero temperatures, a woman's hands became gnarled and misshaped. Because an open-air fire would burn up her hard-won fuel too quickly, she cooked in a low hut that adjoined the snow-house. The woman had to lie on her stomach and constantly blow on the twigs to keep them burning. Sometimes there was no fuel to be found, and the Caribou Eskimos had to make do with frozen meat for days.

The small knife shown above has an iron blade and a handle of walrus tusk. It was probably used by a young girl while learning household skills from her mother.

For the majority of Eskimos, it was the home, whether constructed of snow or sod or skin, that served as the focus of social activity. In the Arctic, a man's greatest joy was to return from the hunt with enough food to sponsor a feast for the other families in his settlement. On such occasions, he might stand at the entrance tunnel to his home shouting, "Come visit me!" The choicest pieces of meat were always reserved for guests. A host typically emptied his larder even as he protested loudly that his offerings were of poor quality and not sufficiently tasty. The guests, on the other hand, would praise him as a great hunter.

An image of a harpooned seal floats in the bowl of a wooden ladle made by a Bering Strait Eskimo. Also made of horn, antler, or bone, such ladles were used for serving and eating by all Eskimo groups.

A legendary ogre called a Kogukhpuk, a symbol of menace to humankind, decorates the bottom of a wooden bowl made by a Yupik Eskimo.

Most of the food eaten in the arctic region was boiled in bucket-shaped vessels made of soapstone or driftwood. Among the Polar Eskimos of Greenland, the greatest delicacy was *maktak,* flakes of narwhal skin that had been allowed to ferment in the family meat cache for several years. Another special treat was *giviak,* which meant literally "something immersed." It consisted of a gutted seal carcass that had been stuffed with starling-size auks. The carcass was then stored until the blubber liquefied and permeated the birds, curing their flesh. Another delicacy was the fluke of a beluga whale. It was a matter of pride for a host to have so much meat that he could allow a visitor's dogs to gorge themselves to the point where they could not eat another mouthful.

Each region had its own rules of etiquette. Guests usually announced their arrival by shouting into the ventilation hole or the entrance tunnel of the host's home. Before entering the main room, they beat their parkas and other outer garments with a piece of bone or wood, called a *tilugtut,* to shake off the snow. Otherwise their animal-skin clothing would become wet and soggy and quickly freeze when they went back outside. Among native Greenlanders, both sexes sat together at feasts, and each guest received an individual portion. The Hudson Bay Inuits, on the other hand, allowed only men to take part in the feasting. The role of the hunter's wife was restricted to serving chunks of boiled meat to the men with a fork made from a caribou antler or walrus rib. As she gave each chunk to her husband, he would grip it in his teeth and cut off the morsel with a knife. He then passed the chunk around the circle and each guest ripped off a piece until the meat was gone. Belching and passing wind were considered clear proof that the food had been satisfying. Should a guest become sleepy, he simply dozed off where he sat and resumed eating when he woke up. Sometimes, after the food had been completely devoured, the party moved to another man's house, where the festivities began all over again. Additional entertainment might be provided by the playing of a one-sided skin drum shaped like a tambourine and beaten with a length of wood or bone. The drummer was often accompanied by another performer who sang and danced, while the audience joined in as a chorus.

Alaskan Eskimos did a great deal of their socializing in community centers known as karigis among the Inupiat and as kashims among the Yupik. Similar in shape to whatever housing style predominated in a particular region, only larger, these buildings brought neighbors together for ceremonial dances, sweat baths, games, and other festivities, or for long nights of storytelling, sometimes illustrated with figurines or "storyknives" of etched ivory. Along the north Alaskan coast, village karigis served essentially as clubhouses for whaling crews, and thus were almost exclusively occupied by males, with women permitted to enter only on special occasions or when delivering meals. Men customarily slept in the karigi, away from their wives. In the fall, the men used the building as a workshop for refurbishing their hunting equipment.

No one went hungry in an Eskimo community if game was available. Eskimo hunters traditionally divided their catch, based on the order in which each man struck the animal. Even men who arrived too late to take part in the kill would symbolically cast their harpoons or spears at the carcass as part of the ritual to claim their share. The first game brought home by young hunters was given away to foster the practice of sharing. Old men too infirm to go along on the hunt might simply spit stones in the direction of the dead animal after it had been dragged back to camp; choice parts of the animal were reserved for them. A Polar Eskimo elder on Saunders Island off the northwest coast of Greenland once explained this sharing concept to the Danish explorer Peter Freuchen, after Freuchen had breached Eskimo custom by thanking his hosts for giving him a part of a walrus they had killed. "You must not thank for your meat," the elder advised. "It is your right to get parts. In this country, nobody wishes to be dependent upon others. There is nobody who gives or gets gifts, for thereby you become dependent."

When a lone hunter succeeded in killing a seal, he presented portions of it to all the other families in the settlement. This custom, known as *payudarpok* by the Polar Eskimos, was based on the Eskimo principle that the wild animals are no one's exclusive property. The responsibility for

PLAYING THE GAME OF STORYKNIVES

In a game played in southwestern Alaska since the 1700s, young Yupik girls spend hours every day telling each other stories—and illustrating the tales by drawing pictures with pointed tools such as the one below called a storyknife.

The game, like many children's pastimes, is bound by rules and conventions. First several girls, sitting in a circle, carefully smooth a small patch of mud or snow between them with their knives or other implements. Then the girl telling the first story begins by sketching a floor plan of an Eskimo home, setting the stage for the drama to come. Next she draws the characters using stylized stick figures *(bottom)* as they arrive on the scene. Characters cannot speak or act until they have been drawn—and must be erased when they leave the scene. When the first girl has finished her tale, another immediately begins, sketching away with her storyknife.

Traditionally, the game is played solely by girls. It provides an absorbing creative outlet as well as a way for them to work out through their made-up dramas the moral and practical lessons—essential to the preservation of Eskimo life and customs—that are taught them by their parents.

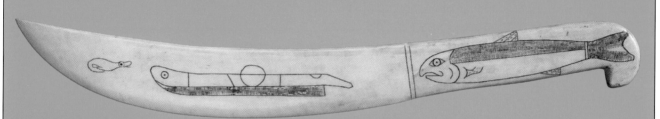

Painted fish swim on the ivory handle and blade of the storyknife above, made in the late 19th century. Now considered valuable keepsakes, old ivory storyknives are seldom used today; other pointed objects are substituted.

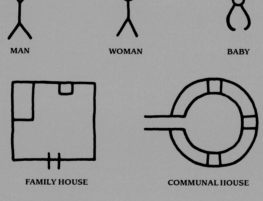

MAN

WOMAN

BABY

FAMILY HOUSE

COMMUNAL HOUSE

SLEEPING IN BED

ANIMAL OR HUMAN TRACKS

TREES

PTARMIGAN SNARE

The symbols that Yupik girls use to describe components of everyday life in telling their tales vary in shape and number from one Alaskan village to another. A selection of the symbols employed by the girls of several southwestern Alaska villages are shown at left.

carrying out payudarpok rested with the wife of the hunter, who took charge of the catch after her husband delivered it to their home. It was considered a great honor for a woman to go around from house to house in the community announcing the good news.

Most Eskimos have always lived in villages or small nomadic bands consisting of a core group of related siblings and their spouses. Membership was quite flexible, however, for a person could join any band in which he or she had a relative. As a result, people frequently traveled with more than one band during the course of a lifetime. Although each band claimed hunting rights to a particular expanse of land, such rights were seldom defended, and bands moved freely from one area to another. They knew, through their oral histories, how they were related to the people of other bands. In winter, kindred groups gathered at sealing camps to share surplus food and goods, arrange marriages, play games, and hold sacred dances and festivals. In the summer, they might meet again for a communal caribou hunt. The end of the summer often found the groups at trading centers where the sea people exchanged their ocean goods of driftwood, whale and seal oil, and walrus tusks for the caribou, fox, wolf, and wolverine skins of the land people.

Neither the northern coastal dwellers nor the inland dwellers had chiefs—although older men with reputations for wisdom, good judgment, and exceptional hunting skills served as informal leaders. The whaling boat captains, or umeliks, of the Inupiat villages along Alaska's northwest coast commanded great respect, for example, but their following did not extend beyond their own family and crew, and they had no political authority. Inland dwellers, such as the Caribou Eskimos, called such a hunt leader an *umealiq,* a word literally meaning "boat owner," but referring here to the stakes used to make a stockade for capturing caribou. The Utkuhikhalingmiut, a subgroup within the Netsilik, called such an individual an *ihumataaq,* or "one who has wisdom." His opinions—when and where to hunt for seals, for example—weighed more than others', although individuals were always free to ignore his advice. Few did, however. A Netsilik man named Akkrak explained how he consulted Ulik, his stepfather and the ihumataaq of his camp, on all travel matters. "If Ulik

Using her ulu, or all-purpose knife, an Inuit hunter's wife carefully butchers the carcass of a caribou on the snow near Bathurst Inlet in Canada's Northwest Territories. Later she will dry much of the meat, preserving it for winter use.

Wood-handled knife to his mouth, an Inuit boy makes a meal by cutting bite-size morsels of raw char. Frequently unable to cook their food while traveling during the winter, Eskimos have long been accustomed to eating uncooked meat and raw fish.

would disapprove of a far travel planned by me, I won't go," Akkrak said. "Such things have happened. Although I sometimes feel a certain fear, I will go if Ulik tells me."

Many camps and villages also had angatkoks, the shamans recognized for their special powers to communicate with the forces of good and evil. Shamans could be called upon to beseech the powers to bring about changes. They might be asked, for example, to induce the moon-man spirit to release the game animals, invoke good luck, and heal the sick by retrieving their stolen souls. In order to become a shaman, a young man underwent many months of training with an elderly angatkok. During his apprenticeship, the youth was required to observe strict food taboos and abstain from sexual relations. He learned the secret language spoken by shamans since ancient times, and he received a special spirit, or *toornaq*, to help him perform his magic. Because shamans could use their power for evil as well as for good, these men—and, in rare cases, women—were as much feared as they were respected.

In contrast with the egalitarian nature of the Eskimos, Aleutian Islanders were highly rank conscious. The social structure of their villages more closely resembled that of their Northwest Coast Indian neighbors, such as the Tlingit, Haida, and Tsimshian. Each Aleut village produced several chiefs, or *toyons,* people of great wealth and prestige who, along

Two young Inuit women of Labrador wear parkas with hoods called amauts that were used to carry children. The circles of white fur on the aprons worn over the parkas—a feature seen only in the arctic areas of eastern Canada—symbolized the womb and indicated the women were of childbearing age.

with other members of the "nobility," ruled over the poorer and less-privileged mass of commoners and slaves. Aleut communities were also organized around a rigid system of family clans, each with its own set of rules and rituals.

With some exceptions, there was no Eskimo equivalent to the Aleut toyon. Instead, authority rested almost exclusively within the nuclear family. With only a few restrictions, individual families were free to come and go as they pleased. The well-being and survival of the family unit depended on the industry and talents of both husband and wife, who worked together as a team. Man and woman were considered incomplete without each other. Among some groups, the word *aippara*, "my spouse," literally meant "my other self." The man hunted and fished, constructed the dwellings, fed the dogs, and made all the weapons and tools, including those that were used by his wife. The woman, on the other hand, performed all of the household duties—cleaning fish, cooking meat, melting ice for drinking water, and making sure the lamps stayed lighted. She also scraped, cut, dried, and cleaned all the animal skins her husband brought back to their home. Most hides were dried and stored away until the woman was ready to process them. To prepare a frozen hide for scraping, she might sleep on it overnight to allow her body heat to loosen the fibers and then soften it further by chewing on it as she worked. The wife made all the clothing, boots, tents, kayak covers, containers, and bedding. On the trail, she also helped lead the dogs and pulled the sled when necessary.

It was an exceptionally demanding existence, centered on the almost daily struggle against cold and hunger. As an Inuit woman told Knud Rasmussen in 1923: "Up here where we live, our life is one continuous fight for food and for clothing and a struggle against bad hunting and snowstorms

Toting her chubby brother on her back in ancient Eskimo fashion, an Inuit girl uses a modern version of the amaut made of woolen cloth. Women of the Arctic still carry their children everywhere, lugging them around until they are able to walk.

and sickness. That is all I can tell you about the world, both the one I know and the one I do not know."

Because men and women depended so heavily on each other for survival, every child was expected to marry as soon as he or she became old enough. A girl's first menses signaled her preparedness for marriage, but a boy could not take on a wife until he had learned to construct an igloo and hunt with enough skill to provide for a family. Only then was a male considered to be a productive member of the community. Among the Aleuts, a boy had to build his own bidarka, or kayak, before he could marry. Most boys did not develop such talents until they were 17 or 18 years of age.

Parents sometimes arranged marriages for their daughters, although a girl was permitted to refuse her parents' choice and select her own husband. In order to reduce the possibility of wedding a lazy housekeeper or a poor hunter, however, most families preferred that their children choose their spouses from a band of people who were well known to them. Among some Eskimo groups, a man was expected to take his bride by force. Even if the girl was willing to marry him, she was obliged to put up at least a token show of resistance.

A strict set of marriage taboos limited the choice of a husband or wife. Among some groups, cousins could not marry one another; nor could step-siblings. Widows and widowers were frequently forbidden to marry any sibling of their dead spouses; nor could two brothers wed two sisters. Yet not all Eskimo peoples shared the same taboos. The Bering Strait Eskimos, for example, permitted marriage between cousins because they believed blood relatives made more trustworthy spouses. When a young Bering Strait man decided on a girl to marry, he informed his mother and father, who then approached the girl's parents to ask for their consent. If the answer was yes, the boy donned his finest clothes and went to the girl's house, where he presented his bride with new garments, meticulously sewn by his mother. The young couple then began living together, either by themselves or with the parents of the husband or wife. Among other groups, the girl's parents made the marriage proposal by presenting a desirable young man with a gift—a knife, perhaps, or a parka. After the marriage, the boy went to work for his parents-in-law, sometimes only as long as it took for him to catch a seal for them. Among other groups, such as

The three Eskimo women above all wear tattoos that, along with other facial decorations, were long thought to vastly enhance female beauty. Such tattoos usually signified a woman's readiness to marry and bear children.

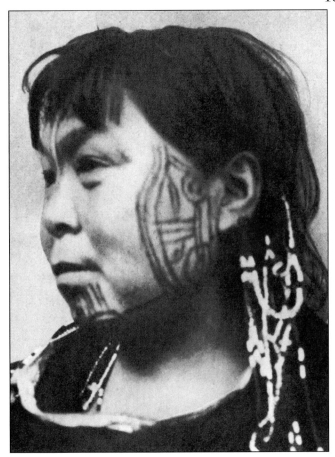

the Copper Eskimos, a man simply built a shelter and invited the bride of his choice to move in with him. Most marriages were not recognized as fully legitimate until the couple produced children.

A woman could divorce her husband at any time simply by leaving their house. Usually she returned to her parents, taking a few belongings and her children, if any, with her. A man could similarly divorce his wife, although if the wife demanded it, he would be obliged to continue supporting her, making a separate dwelling for her whenever their camp shifted to a new location and providing her with a continual supply of skins, blubber, and meat. Although Eskimo societies did not frown on polygamy, very few men took on more than one wife because of the extra responsibilities it required. A wife having two husbands was even more rare.

Wife exchanges under very formalized conditions, on the other hand, sometimes occurred, particularly between couples whose men had developed a "song partnership," a special type of friendship unique to Eskimo society. Song partners, or *idloreet,* usually belonged to separate camps and were not related. They traveled to different hunting grounds throughout most of the year but renewed their friendship when they came together in the winter camps. To demonstrate their close ties publicly, the men would stage an elaborate drum dance in the large ceremonial igloo. The festivities began with the song partners standing in the middle of the room, holding each other by the waist, rubbing noses, and shouting joyful cries

Sewing clothes the old way, Minnie Al-lakaraluk of Canada's Resolute Bay uses sinew to stitch caribou skin into a traditional winter outfit. Eskimo women keep their sewing gear in supple leather bags, like the one above made of caribou ears, that can be rolled up and tied with an ivory-tipped thong fastener.

Safeguarding their
sewing needles, Es-
kimo women use in-
genious cases such
as the ivory tube at
right carved like a
seal with a stopper
at one end. Other
cases consist of
open-ended tubes of
copper and ivory
(left and below)
holding needles
stuck to sealskin
strips that pull out.

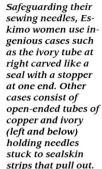

of welcome to the audience. One of their wives began chanting a song composed especially for the occasion and taught to her earlier by her husband. Other women joined in with the refrain, while the soloist's husband danced slowly in circles, beating a drum. After the song ended, the song partners would embrace again, and the drum would be passed to the second man, who then danced while his wife sang. Later in the night, the two men would exchange wives, thus cementing their new relationship.

On other occasions, a wife exchange might be a matter of simple practicality. A man might need to go on a prolonged hunting trip, for example, but find that his own wife was unable to accompany him because of illness or pregnancy. He would then take along his neighbor's wife, leaving his own with the neighbor. It was essential to a hunter's success to have a woman along. Without a woman to dry his clothing, soften his boots by chewing the soles, melt fresh water, boil meat, and process hides, hunting became more difficult and less productive.

Most wife exchanges were of short duration. In some cases, however, the swap became permanent. Exchanges were usually arranged by the husbands. The women seldom objected; most wives considered it an honor to be desired by other men. Sometimes they even suggested the exchange themselves. Yet while the Eskimos sometimes considered it natural for a man or woman to want more than one sex partner, they also had strict rules to control promiscuity. When several families had to occupy the same house, for example, the men and boys were expected to sleep as far away as possible from the women and girls.

Young aggressive men sometimes abducted married women they desired for themselves. With the assistance of sympathetic relatives—and sometimes of the woman herself—the abductor would drag a woman to his house and hold her captive. Such an abduction could happen at any time and frequently involved a fierce struggle between the husband and his rival.

The husband of an abducted wife had several options. He could attempt to get her back by force, a course of action that often ended in bloodshed and a long, bitter feud between the kin of the two men. Or he could decide to let the other man keep his wife in exchange for some form of compensation—a few sealskins, perhaps, or some meat. He could also choose to ignore the situation and wait to see if his wife returned to him. Far from becoming the laughingstock of the community, a man who took no action was considered patient and magnanimous—two honored traits among Eskimo peoples. His reputation rose

Aleut housewife Frances Usugan holds a double arm-load of dried and inflated seal intestine. Lengths of seal gut, slit and stitched together, make superb waterproof parkas, essential clothing for Aleut seal hunters venturing out to sea in kayaks.

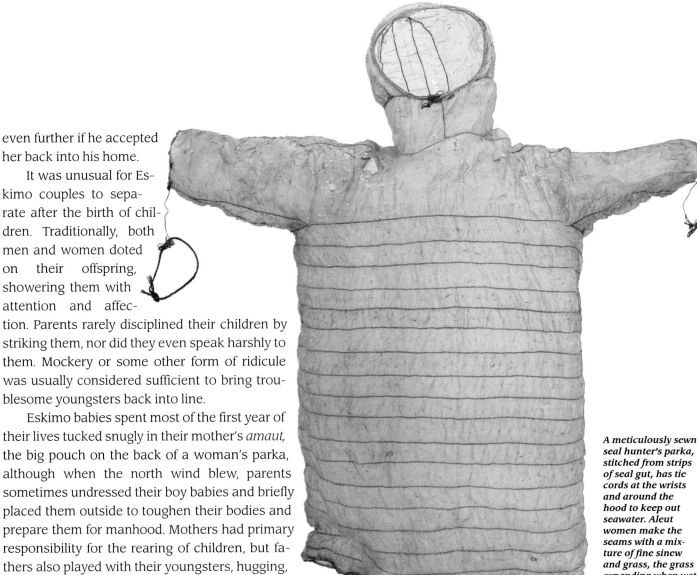

even further if he accepted her back into his home.

It was unusual for Eskimo couples to separate after the birth of children. Traditionally, both men and women doted on their offspring, showering them with attention and affection. Parents rarely disciplined their children by striking them, nor did they even speak harshly to them. Mockery or some other form of ridicule was usually considered sufficient to bring troublesome youngsters back into line.

Eskimo babies spent most of the first year of their lives tucked snugly in their mother's *amaut,* the big pouch on the back of a woman's parka, although when the north wind blew, parents sometimes undressed their boy babies and briefly placed them outside to toughen their bodies and prepare them for manhood. Mothers had primary responsibility for the rearing of children, but fathers also played with their youngsters, hugging, cuddling, and rubbing noses with them. As the children grew older, the parent-child relationship became more restrained, although it remained loving. At the age of four or five, boys began following their fathers about the camp, watching and studying everything they did. Fathers, in turn, made miniature weapons and sleds for their sons, and encouraged them to play at hunting. Sometimes young girls joined the boys in these games, tying antlers to their heads while the boys pretended to track them down. When boys reached the age of about 10 or 11, they began to assist their fathers on hunting and fishing trips.

Eskimo girls learned their duties from their mothers. By the age of seven or so, girls ceased their playing and began to help their mothers gather tundra plants and moss or cut ice for drinking water. Mothers encouraged young daughters to make clothes for their dolls and to mend their own clothing, teaching them how to cut out the skins and do the stitching. They also gave their daughters tiny cooking lamps with which to "play

A meticulously sewn seal hunter's parka, stitched from strips of seal gut, has tie cords at the wrists and around the hood to keep out seawater. Aleut women make the seams with a mixture of fine sinew and grass, the grass expanding when wet to make the parka totally waterproof.

house" in a corner of the family igloo. By age 10, most girls were proficient homemakers and often carried infant siblings around on their backs.

Adoption was common in Eskimo communities. It usually took place within the extended family—a couple might adopt a nephew, for example, or an older woman might adopt a grandchild—but the adoption of nonrelated children, particularly by childless couples, also occurred. Most adopted children had been either orphaned or born into an impoverished family. Parents wishing to place a child for adoption sought prosperous couples with a reputation for kindness and modesty. All adoptions were permanent; parents who later demanded the return of a relinquished child faced the scorn of their community.

Yet despite the Eskimo love of children, the harsh day-to-day demands of arctic life and ever-present threat of starvation frequently led to the practice of infanticide. Girls were killed more often than boys because of their inability to hunt and fish—and thus provide food and a better chance of survival for the family. Infants were usually killed by exposing them to the cold. Sometimes a mother would simply suffocate her unwanted baby with an animal skin immediately after its birth. In times of extreme hardship, abandonment of older family members who were too old, sick, or infirm to contribute to the welfare of the family also occurred. Old women were also sometimes killed after being accused of practicing witchcraft. Occasionally, elders who felt that they had become a burden to their family committed suicide.

Infanticide seldom happened after a baby received his or her *atiq*, or "name soul." Although the atiq served as an individual's name, the Eskimos considered it much more. It represented the spirit, now embodied in the infant, of a beloved older relative who had died, frequently a grandparent, or a granduncle or grandaunt. Infants received their atiq when they were a few days old. Parents examined their newborns carefully for birthmarks, mannerisms, or physical traits that might provide a clue as to whose atiq resided within the child. As they grew older, children often acquired nicknames that superseded the atiq given them at birth. Since all names possessed power and acted as guardian spirits for the individual bearing them, most Eskimo men and women tried to acquire as many as possible. Some Netsiliks had as many as 12 names.

In general, the Eskimo peoples marked the passage from childhood into adulthood not with public ceremonies, as was the custom among many other Native American groups, but rather in less formal ways. In northern Alaska, boys donned different clothing once their voices began

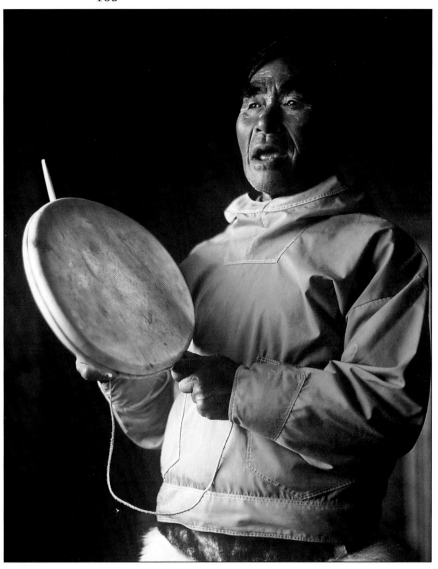

A Polar Eskimo named Massautsiaq sings a song while striking the rim of a traditional flat, tambourine-like drum. Skin drums, usually made of walrus gut, and box drums made of wood are the only musical instruments native to the Arctic.

to change. But the true sign that full adulthood had been achieved among males came with the piercing of the lower lip for labrets, decorative plugs made from shell, ivory, sandstone, wood, and other materials. No particular ceremony attended this event. When a father decided his son was ready to assume the duties and privileges of manhood, he enlisted the aid of a man skilled in performing such operations. The man made the necessary cuts by quickly driving a stone knife through the flesh just under each corner of the boy's mouth. To prove his manhood, the boy could not cry out or show any sign of pain. Once a young man began wearing labrets, he was free to seek sexual partners or marry.

Eskimo girls commonly announced their eligibility for marriage by having their faces tattooed. An older woman, often a relative, did the tattooing, pulling a needle and thread that had been drawn through the soot of an oil lamp into and out of the young girl's chin. The most common tattoo design consisted of a series of closely drawn parallel lines that ran from the center of the lower lip to the base of the chin. Many girls also had their ears, nose, or lips pierced so they could wear special dangling pendants made of beads, bone, and cloth.

During their first menses, Eskimo girls were confined to their family's house, or sometimes to a separate birth hut, if one had already been erected nearby. In some areas of northern Alaska, girls wore a special hood of caribou skin for the duration of their first menstrual period to protect their eyes from sunlight, which was believed to be harmful to them at that time. They also were required to obey certain restrictions. They could not eat, or even touch, red meat, for example, nor drink from any container other than a special menstrual cup.

Because in some communities so many girl babies were killed at birth, there was often a shortage of women in Eskimo villages. Competition for wives often led to intense jealousies and deep distrust between male rivals. Even men who had traveled and hunted together for years remained cautiously alert at all times, fearful that one of their companions might suddenly thrust a knife between their shoulder blades. Many a man died at

Two Greenlanders in the settlement of Angmagssalik look each other squarely in the face in a rare 1906 photograph of a song duel—a contest widely used to settle personal disputes. Typically, each opponent sang verses ridiculing the other, while several fellow villagers observed and pronounced the victor. The loser was expected to accept defeat gracefully—or leave town.

This wooden mask from eastern Greenland was worn by contestants during ritualistic song duels. Masks not only looked fearsome but also afforded protection when rival singers decided to make head butting part of the contest.

the hand of a longtime acquaintance who secretly coveted his wife or who harbored resentment for his superior kayaking or seal-hunting skills. For this reason, some Eskimo men used to carry two knives with them at all times, one on each side under their parkas, which they could pull out quickly in the event of a sudden argument.

Tempers became particularly taut during the long, dark winter months, a time when even the most trivial of disputes could spark an explosion of violence. The Canadian ethnographer Diamond Jenness witnessed a murder in the winter of 1915 when he was living among the Copper Eskimos. According to Jenness, a Kanghiryuak on Victoria Island "was sitting in his hut sharpening a knife that he had just made, when a neighbor entered and began to jeer at him, saying that he did not know how to make a knife. The owner quietly continued to sharpen his weapon until its edge was keen enough, then drove it into the jester's stomach with the remark, 'Now see if I can't make a knife.' "

The male kin of an Eskimo murder victim were entitled to seek revenge, by killing either the murderer or one of the murderer's close relatives. This usually ended the matter, although sometimes the incident

At a Mask Dance.

Five men in the foreground, wearing gauntlets and feather headdresses, perform the traditional Wolf Dance in a drawing made by an Alaskan artist in the 1890s. Behind them a chorus of women wave feather wands and sway to the rhythm of drums. The Wolf Dance was part of the Messenger Feast, a yearly winter festival.

erupted into a bitter feud that spewed violence for generations to come. For other, lesser crimes—theft, for example, or destruction of property—Eskimos developed several ways of settling the matter. Among the Netsilik, for instance, any man who believed he had been wronged could challenge an opponent to a fistfight. The match proceeded according to a strict protocol. The two men stripped to the waist, then took turns punching each other, but only one blow at a time and only to the opponent's temple or shoulder. Neither man could defend himself when it was his turn to be hit. The fight—and the dispute that triggered it—ended when one of the men either gave up or became severely injured.

Another, less physical method of resolving a feud involved a public song duel, an aggressive version of the friendly song partner ceremony that was part of formalized wife swapping. These songs, however, were anything but cordial. In the song duel, each man used derisive lyrics and suggestive dance movements in an effort to humiliate his opponent. Each party might accuse the other of committing various disgraceful acts, from being henpecked and a poor hunter to engaging in incest, bestiality, and murder. The more biting and witty the song, the more the onlookers roared their approval. The winner of the song duel was the man with the larger inventory of insulting ditties.

From time to time, an individual would exhibit such dangerous aggression that an entire community sanctioned his or her execution. A person might become mentally deranged, for example, acting in an increasingly strange and menacing manner. Or a shaman might become angry and bitter, misusing his powers against even his closest relatives to cause illness or a shortage of food. Such antisocial behavior threatened the security of the camp and could not be tolerated for long. In these instances,

Long sealskin gauntlets worn by festival dancers are encrusted with puffin beaks that rattle. Wearing ceremonial mittens emphasized hand movements—and warded off evil spirits. Above the gauntlets are woman's waving wands made of eagle feathers and tipped with eagle down.

the relatives of the offending person might gather and decide if the situation warranted the death sentence. If they agreed that it did, one of them would be assigned the task. By having a close relative carry out the execution, there would be no cause for revenge.

One of the last known incidents of a sanctioned Eskimo murder occurred in 1922 among a group of Netsiliks camped in the vicinity of Pelly Bay. A young man named Arnaktark, who had been suffering for a period of several months from a mental disturbance, suddenly stabbed his wife in the stomach. She fled on foot with their young child to her in-laws' house and told them what had happened. "They started to fear that he might stab again at someone they loved," Arnaktark's nephew, Kringorn, 16 years old at the time, related to anthropologist Asen Balikci. "The discussion was held among family, and it was felt that Arnaktark, because he had become a danger to them, should be killed." Arnaktark's oldest brother, Kokonwatsiark, volunteered to do the killing, and the others agreed. The family broke camp, moving the women and children to a location farther down the coast. Kokonwatsiark, accompanied by several other male relatives, including his aging father, then went to Arnaktark's house. They found the crazed man standing outside. "Kokonwatsiark said to him, 'Because you do not know very well anymore, I am going to have you,' " Kringorn recalled. "Then he aimed at his heart and shot him through the chest." After moving Arnaktark's body to the shore of a nearby lake, the men continued on to join their families at the new camp.

Temporary bouts of insanity, or "Arctic hysteria," were not uncommon among the Eskimos. Known as *pibloktoq*, these episodes struck some European explorers as well, frequently with little or no warning. Although the symptoms varied, most afflicted people tore off all or most of their clothing, no matter what the weather, and ran about shouting incomprehensible or obscene words. Some victims imitated the movements and sounds of animals. Many exhibited supernatural strength. In rare cases, people became violent, fighting off anyone who tried to subdue them. A pibloktoq often ended with the victim weeping uncontrollably, then collapsing into a long, deep sleep. Upon awakening, most people remembered nothing of the episode or of their aberrant behavior during it.

Scientists have proposed various explanations for the cause of Arctic hysteria, ranging from the stress of life in the extreme

North to vitamin and mineral deficiencies. Traditionally, the Eskimos claimed that pibloktoq was a physical manifestation of the many invisible spirits that inhabited their world. These supernatural beings took many shapes and forms, from the benevolent souls of dead relatives to bloodthirsty monsters, dwarfs, and giants. Among the most important were the personal souls, or inyusuq, the powerful forces that resided within individuals and served as the source of good health, stamina, will power, and energy—all the elements that gave a person life. These differed from the name souls of deceased relatives that parents bequeathed to their infants after birth. Unlike name souls, personal souls were unique to each individual and journeyed to one of the three Eskimo afterworlds after death, where they dwelt for eternity. Eskimos believed that when a person became ill, it was because evil spirits had entered the body and attacked the inyusuq. To drive out the evil spirits, healthy people sometimes loaned some of their own inyusuq to ailing friends or relatives. For example, if a man complained of severe stomach pain, a friend might try to drive away the illness by spitting on his hand and rubbing the saliva—which contained part of his own vital inyusuq—onto the sick man's abdomen.

If relatives did not adhere to certain taboos after a person's death, the soul became enraged and malicious. This dark, angry spirit, known to some Eskimos as a person's shade, or *tarrak,* was thought to linger near the burial site of the body that it once occupied, refusing to enter the afterworld. It posed a serious threat to the living, for a dead man's tarrak often prowled the tundra, waiting for the opportunity to steal the soul of an unwitting passerby, who would then waste away and die.

Other important spirits resided in the wide variety of amulets that all Eskimo men, women, and children carried around with them. Almost any object could serve as an amulet, from small figures of men or animals carved out of bone or ivory to the teeth, claws, feet, skin, noses, and other dismembered parts of animals. Sometimes an entire stuffed body of a small animal, such as a lemming or squirrel, was used. Each of these charms had a distinctive spirit with specific powers—to keep the harpoon steady during a polar bear hunt, for example, or to protect against headaches. Amulets were frequently obtained from other people, generally from an older respected relative or a shaman. Only the person who owned them could benefit from their power, which grew stronger with time. Most Eskimos either sewed their amulets directly onto their clothing or wore them dangling from special belts. It was not uncommon to own half a dozen or

THE BALEFUL TUPILAK

Most frightening of all creatures in the ancient mythology of the Greenland Inuits are the grotesque and dangerous demons called *tupilek* (plural of *tupilak*) thought to be created by shamans as a means of doing away with their enemies. After combining parts of dead animals and humans, the sorcerers sang special charm songs in order to bring the monsters to life. Once animated, the tupilek would lie in wait under the ice, sneak up on victims by swimming through the sea, flying through the air, or creeping along the ground. Some tupilek were so evil that they terrorized the shamans who made them.

Tales of tupilek fascinated Greenland's Danish settlers, who asked the Inuits what these frightening creatures looked like. The Inuits obliged with grotesque drawings and carvings of tupilek in action. In time, a market for these native artworks developed, and they became collector's items, especially the carvings—which are still being made by gifted Greenlandic artists.

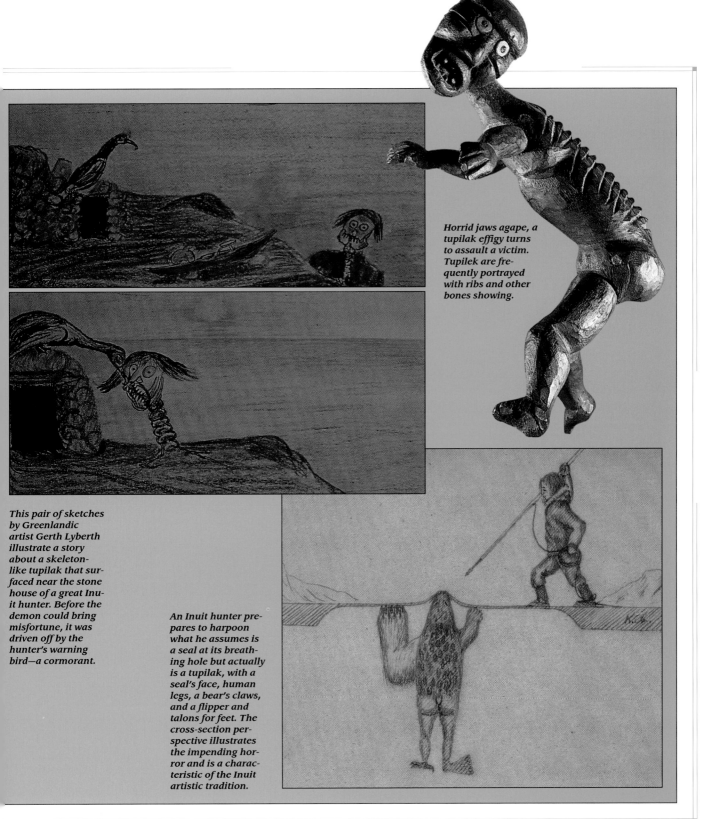

Horrid jaws agape, a tupilak effigy turns to assault a victim. Tupilek are frequently portrayed with ribs and other bones showing.

This pair of sketches by Greenlandic artist Gerth Lyberth illustrate a story about a skeleton-like tupilak that surfaced near the stone house of a great Inuit hunter. Before the demon could bring misfortune, it was driven off by the hunter's warning bird—a cormorant.

An Inuit hunter prepares to harpoon what he assumes is a seal at its breathing hole but actually is a tupilak, with a seal's face, human legs, a bear's claws, and a flipper and talons for feet. The cross-section perspective illustrates the impending horror and is a characteristic of the Inuit artistic tradition.

Yupik women of southwestern Alaska wore small fans on their fingers as they danced during ceremonies. The finger fans at far left are decorated with feathers; those at left are incised with walrus faces.

more personal amulets. Knud Rasmussen told of meeting a young Netsilik man in a camp on Boothia Peninsula who had sewn six amulets into various parts of his clothing: seal teeth to bring him luck when sealing, a tern's head for salmon fishing, a stuffed ermine to make him a good runner, two tiny snow-beaters to protect him against evil spirits, and to improve his kayaking skills, a small tool for cleaning kayaks that had once belonged to a man famous for his fast paddling.

The Eskimos also shared their world with numerous mysterious and often humanlike beings, from tiny mischievous dwarfs to huge cannibalistic ogres. A large repository of stories and legends surrounded these creatures. Most Inuit and Yupik peoples, for example, believed in little beings, about one foot high, who dressed in tiny parkas and sealskin or caribou trousers, and lived in underground houses along the seashore. Other groups told stories of coming across the huge imprints of giants. These evasive goliaths included a race of bears known as the Nanorluk, with jaws so huge that they could swallow men whole, and a woman named Amayersuk, who kidnapped errant children.

In the central and eastern Arctic areas, a sea goddess known variously as Sedna, Nuliajuk, and Takanakapsaluk ruled over all the lesser spirits and monsters. Many Eskimos considered her the mother of both land and sea creatures and, thus, the provider of all life. Another all-pervasive spirit resided in the air and was generally called Sila. In 1923 when Knud Rasmussen lived among the Iglulik of Baffin Bay, he once asked a shaman

Kneeling in front of a chorus of women, Edward Aguchak waves hand fans made of feathers attached to wooden hoops during a performance by his Alaskan troupe, the Scammon Bay dancers. Men knelt in many Eskimo dances and swayed to drum music with precise motions of the torso and arms.

named Aua for an explanation of Sila. The wise man looked out over the wind-swept landscape and responded with a question of his own: "In order to hunt well and live happily, man must have calm weather. Why this constant succession of blizzards and all this needless hardship for men seeking food for themselves and those they care for? Why? Why?"

When Rasmussen could not answer, Aua led him to the snowhouse of a man named Kuvdlo. Inside, Kuvdlo's wife and children huddled together in the dark. "Why should it be cold and comfortless in here?" Aua asked Rasmussen. "Kuvdlo has been out hunting all day, and if he had got a seal, as he deserved, his wife would now be sitting laughing beside her lamp, letting it burn full, without fear of having no blubber left for tomorrow. The place would be warm and bright and cheerful, the children would come out from under their rugs and enjoy life. Why should it not be so? Why?"

Again Rasmussen had no answer. Aua went on to show the ethnogra-

In the main picture, a painted pole topped with a wooden grave image with inlaid ivory eyes (also inset) stands next to a plank box holding the body of a villager in a 1921 photograph taken at Hooper Bay, Alaska. Believing that the spirit lived on after death, Eskimos also honored the deceased by leaving useful worldly goods at grave sites, such as the paddle, bucket, and teapot seen above. At right, a 19th-century watercolor pictures followers of Greenland religious leader Habakuk performing more elaborate rites by dancing around the graves of sect members.

pher other examples in the Iglulik camp of wretchedness brought about by poor luck at sealing. "You see," he said, "you are equally unable to give any reason when we ask you why life is as it is. And so it must be. All our customs come from life and turn towards life; we explain nothing, we believe nothing, but in what I have just shown you lies answer to all you ask. We fear the weather spirit of earth, that we must fight against to wrest our food from land and sea. We fear Sila. We fear death and hunger in the cold snow huts. Therefore it is that our fathers have inherited from their fathers all the old rules of life, which are based on the experience and wisdom of generations. We do not know how, we cannot say why, but we keep those rules in order that we may live untroubled. We have customs, which are not the same as those of the white men, the white men who live in another land and have need of other ways."

These old rules that helped provide protection from the wrath of Sila and the other assorted powers involved numerous taboos and rituals. Various sacred practices governed most of the central activities of Eskimo life—hunting, cooking, and eating—and reflected a strong belief that the very separate worlds of land and sea should not intermingle. Among many groups, it was taboo to serve the flesh of land and sea animals during the same meal, or to use the same weapons to kill them. Before hunting caribou in the spring, some coastal dwellers had to scrub all seal grease accumulated during the winter from their bodies; later, when the whaling season began, they had to wash again and don new clothes that were free of all caribou scent.

Many of the strictest taboos concerned seal, caribou, and bear. To avoid offending a newly killed seal, tradition held that fresh snow had to be scattered on the igloo floor before the animal's carcass could be brought indoors, and that no woman could do any other work in the house until it had been butchered. To keep the soul of a slaughtered caribou from turning into an evil spirit, the animal's ears could not be severed from its carcass while it was being skinned, nor could its meat be cooked over driftwood gathered from the sea. In deference to the spirit of the brown bear, some north Alaskan groups forbade women to eat its flesh. Men could feast on the bear meat, but they had to wear old clothes and abstain from sexual intercourse for the following several days, until the bear's soul moved peacefully to the afterworld.

Childbirth had its own set of rules. To ensure a small baby—and thus an easier delivery—pregnant women sometimes wore straps around their bodies and avoided certain foods. They also kept their distance from other pregnant women and dressed in old clothes that could be discarded—along with their impurities—immediately after the birth. In most villages and camps, women delivered their babies in small huts built by their husbands especially for the event. An older female relative sometimes aided with the delivery, and in a few communities, the father was permitted to watch. Netsilik women, however, gave birth without any assistance, for their communities deemed women in labor too impure to be touched. Inupiat shamans, who risked losing their power if they came in direct contact with a pregnant woman, helped out by drumming and chanting strength-giving songs from the safe distance of a nearby house.

Most Eskimo women delivered their babies while kneeling on a bed of dried moss. After the baby was born, the mother or her midwife cut the umbilical cord with a special flint knife held in the left hand. She then carefully wrapped the placenta in animal skins, which someone later buried outside in a place safe from dogs and other animals. If any creature disturbed the placenta, misfortune would befall the child. After wiping her newborn with a special piece of animal skin, which immediately became one of the child's most powerful amulets, the mother applied a diaper of moss and caribou skins and tucked the infant into the hood of her parka. Some Eskimo mothers nursed their babies immediately; others fed them water mixed with oil or melted blubber for a day or two first. The mother remained in the birth hut with her newborn for four or five days, eating only meat from animals with characteristics she desired for her child. A woman who wished her son to grow up to be a good runner and kayaker might consume nothing but duck wings while in isolation. Babies received their name souls after they left the birth hut.

When someone died, another strict set of taboos had to be followed, lest the dead person's soul turn into an evil tarrak and bring harm to the community. It was believed that a soul remained in its body for four or five days following death. Among the Netsilik, during this period, no member of the immediate family of the deceased could do any kind of work, and others in the camp were required to refrain from combing their hair, cutting their nails, feeding their dogs, driving their sleds, and cleaning their soapstone lamps. When the mourning period ended, two relatives placed the body on a sled, drove it some distance from the camp, and left it on the ice. If a person died while inland during the summer months, a stone might be placed at the head of the body and another at its feet. Relatives always moved on to a new camp after depositing a body—just in case an angry tarrak lingered near the grave site. ◆▢◆

EMISSARY TO THE GODS

According to Eskimo legend, the people of the harsh arctic lands once lived in a gentler world where food grew plentifully and humans flourished. But in time the earth grew cold and barren, and many people died. It was then, say the Iglulik Eskimos, that one man suddenly felt the mysterious urge to dive into the earth. The ground parted beneath him like water, and down he plunged until he reached the subterranean deity, Mother of Sea Beasts. She gave him game, which he took back to humankind, ending the famine and saving his people.

That man, in Iglulik tradition, was the first shaman, the pivotal figure in maintaining the precarious balance of life in a harsh environment. Shamans guided their communities in appeasing and otherwise dealing with the potentially destructive spirits that populated the earth. And they acted as intermediaries between the human and spirit worlds, regularly pleading with the deities to intercede on behalf of humankind whenever things went awry despite the elaborate taboos, offerings, and other preventive measures people undertook. "If I cannot manage in spite of all these precautions, and suffer want or sickness," a Netsilik Eskimo explained to explorer Knud Rasmussen, "I must seek help from the shamans whose mission it is to be the protectors of mankind against all the hidden forces and dangers of life."

A shaman wears a wooden mask and gloves to protect him from malevolent forces as he tries to cure a sick boy. An amulet belt like the one hung with tiny horn knives (top) was usually the sole insignia of a shaman's rank.

THE EASE OF FLIGHT

Traditional shamans, according to Eskimo accounts, possessed vast and extraordinary powers. They could shake the earth, walk on clouds, make themselves invisible, raise the dead, and give off sparks from their own bodies. But of all their powers, none was greater or more essential to their role than their ability to fly. Shamans regularly flew off to visit the deities, to retrieve lost souls, to obtain information, or sometimes just for the fun of it, circling the globe or soaring to the moon and stars in the joyous exercise of their powers.

People frequently reported seeing shamans in flight, and their faith in shamanic tales of far-off places was unshakable. Anthropologist Vilhjalmur Stefansson once described the moon's cratered surface as seen through telescopes to several Eskimos. They replied politely that the white man's information was at odds with their own—obtained, they added, from men who had actually been to the moon. And, as Stefansson later wrote, "They thought that under the circumstances, the Eskimos ought to be better informed."

Tiny figures from an ivory engraving depict a shaman taking flight through the walls of a ceremonial dwelling. Inside, a helper beats a drum, creating the rhythmic sound that helped induce flight.

Animal familiars fly with a shaman in a drawing by an Eskimo. Shamans were frequently accompanied in flight by such spirit helpers, or the shaman himself might assume the guise of an animal—sometimes even sprouting the wings of a bird.

Worn by an Iglulik shaman named Qingailisaq (right), an unusual hoodless coat (shown front and back) with separate hat and mittens depicts in various symbols an encounter he once had with mountain spirits. The white hands sewn on the front of the garment are to fend off evil spirits.

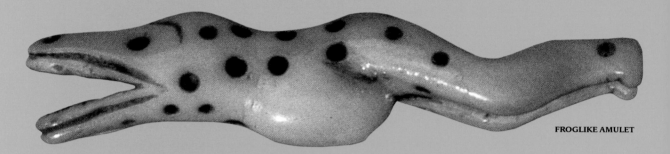

FROGLIKE AMULET

A HOST OF SHAMAN HELPERS

In order to deal effectively with evil forces and the major deities, all shamans relied on the aid of inuas, the spiritual occupants that resided in all things—living or inanimate. So important were these spirit helpers that in some parts of Alaska a shaman was referred to simply as "one who has spirits." Typically, spirit helpers took the form of animal familiars or animal-like beings, such as those pictured here. They assisted a shaman in many ways: as a source of power for fantastic deeds such as flight, as aides in communicating with the ruling spirits, and as informants who observed broken taboos within the community.

Shamans pleased and flattered their spirit helpers by creating amulets in their image. Some amulets were endowed with broad beneficial powers. Others were employed for specific practical purposes, such as aiding hunters in their pursuit of game or sailing with fishermen to keep their kayaks seaworthy. But whatever their specific properties, each amulet derived its potency from the spirit it represented.

CARVING OF A YOUNG WALRUS

FOX-SKIN HAND PUPPET

IVORY POLAR BEAR

EMPLOYING THE POWER TO HEAL

Because Eskimos believed that the source of all illness was spiritual, one of a shaman's major tasks was to cure the sick. A variety of techniques existed, depending on whether the malady was caused by the machinations of evil beings, by the loss of a person's soul, or in retaliation for violated taboos.

Healing took place during a public ceremony. The shaman called upon the sick person to confess to breaking taboos and then encouraged the audience to help him placate the disease-causing spirits by furnishing excuses for the transgressions. In those instances in which malevolent spirits had entered a person's body, a shaman might lick, suck, or blow on the diseased part to extract the offending element, then attack it with a knife and fling it into the fire or feed it to a dog. If a shaman determined that a disease was caused by a soul's having wandered off or having been stolen from its body, he would send spirit helpers after it, or fly off to retrieve it himself.

In conjunction with these spiritual remedies, shamans also possessed practical medical skills to use when appropriate: applying fat to burns, using urine to clean wounds, amputating frozen or gangrenous limbs, lancing infections, and setting broken bones.

Employing the same diagnostic technique depicted on the ivory engraving (above), a shaman lifts a patient's head in a strap (right) while questioning a spirit about the disease. As long as a shaman could hold the head up, the answers to the questions were deemed to be negative; if the head became too heavy to hold, the spirit had answered in the affirmative.

A drum (left) decorated with animal teeth and human hair is fitted to a handle carved in the shape of a human with exposed ribs and internal organs. Shamans used such drums to summon spirits for curing ceremonies.

In a trance state, a shaman in bindings embarks on a journey to the nether world in search of a sick person's soul. Shamans were bound to prevent their spirit helpers from flying away.

IMAGES FROM THE NETHER WORLD

The fabulous mythological creatures that Eskimo shamans encountered in dreams or in the course of their flights to the spirit world were rendered tangible to their communities in the form of the masks that were used in ceremonial dances. Created either by the shaman himself, or by a skilled craftsman in accordance with the shaman's instructions, these colorful and imaginative masks represent the powerful deities believed to control natural phenomena or the spirits, or inuas, of game animals and other creatures.

Masks generally were carved from wood and ranged in size from lightweight face coverings to massive constructions as tall as a person. The latter, too heavy to be worn, were suspended from the ceilings of ceremonial houses. Masks were designed according to individual impulse and inspiration, and no two were exactly alike. Many of them, however, incorporated artistic conventions that identified them as specific beings, such as *tungat* (plural of *tungak*), the spirits who controlled the supply of game animals. Tungat were frequently depicted with motifs suggesting the moon, where they were said to reside. When a shaman wore a mask, its spirit was thought to dwell within him, conferring its special powers. Most masks were used for only a single performance or celebration. Then, their powers having been exhausted, they were burned, buried, or sometimes sold.

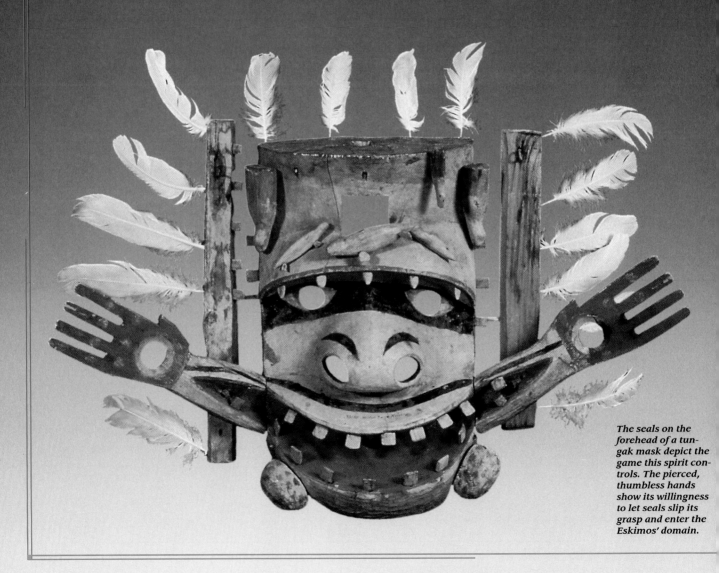

The seals on the forehead of a tungak mask depict the game this spirit controls. The pierced, thumbless hands show its willingness to let seals slip its grasp and enter the Eskimos' domain.

The eyes of this mask, one round, the other a crescent, suggest phases of the moon, the realm where the tungat are believed to reside. The paint-splattered face indicates a recent bloody meal.

DEITIES OF WIND AND WATER

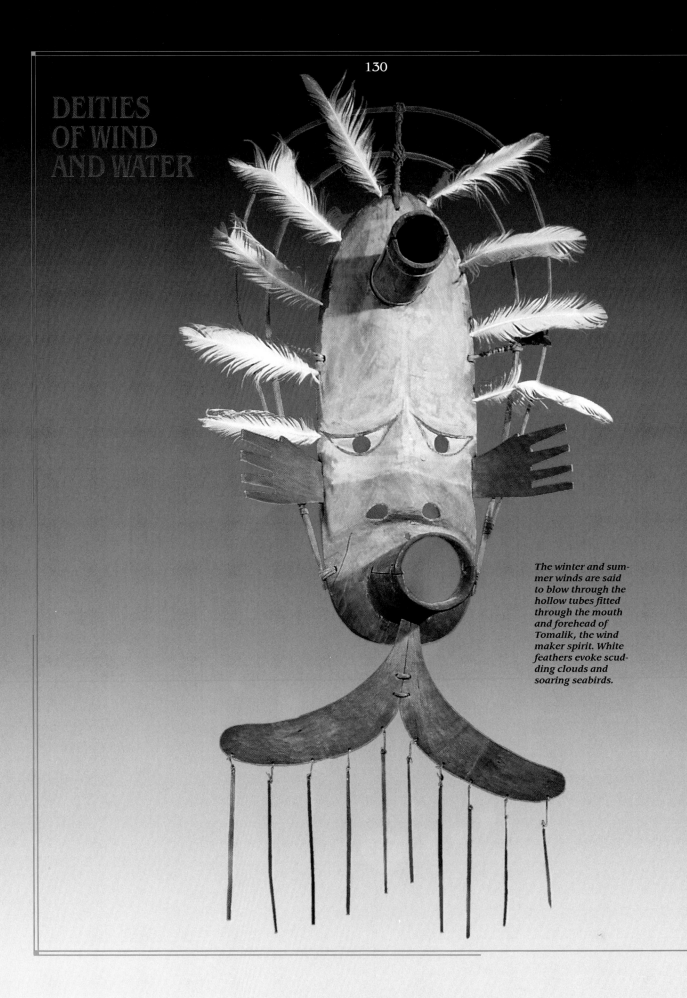

The winter and summer winds are said to blow through the hollow tubes fitted through the mouth and forehead of Tomalik, the wind maker spirit. White feathers evoke scudding clouds and soaring seabirds.

The water deity *Walaunuk* wears a curved tube with wooden disks that represent air bubbles. Eskimos observed the air bubbles that rose to the surface from seal bladders ceremonially submerged; they foretold success or failure in hunting and fishing.

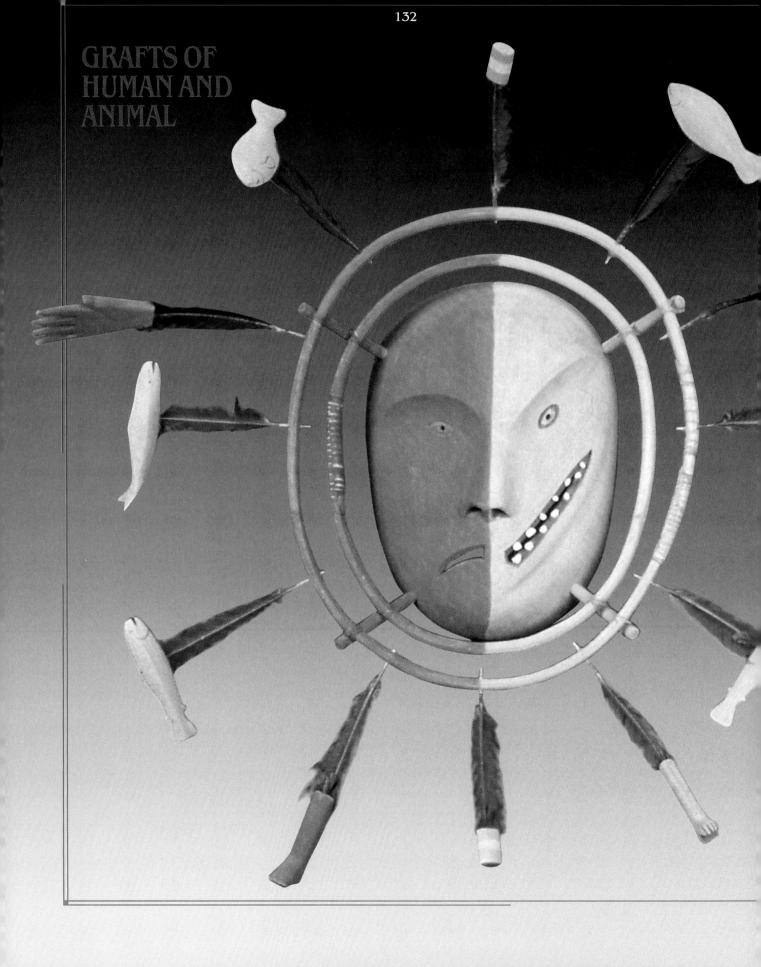

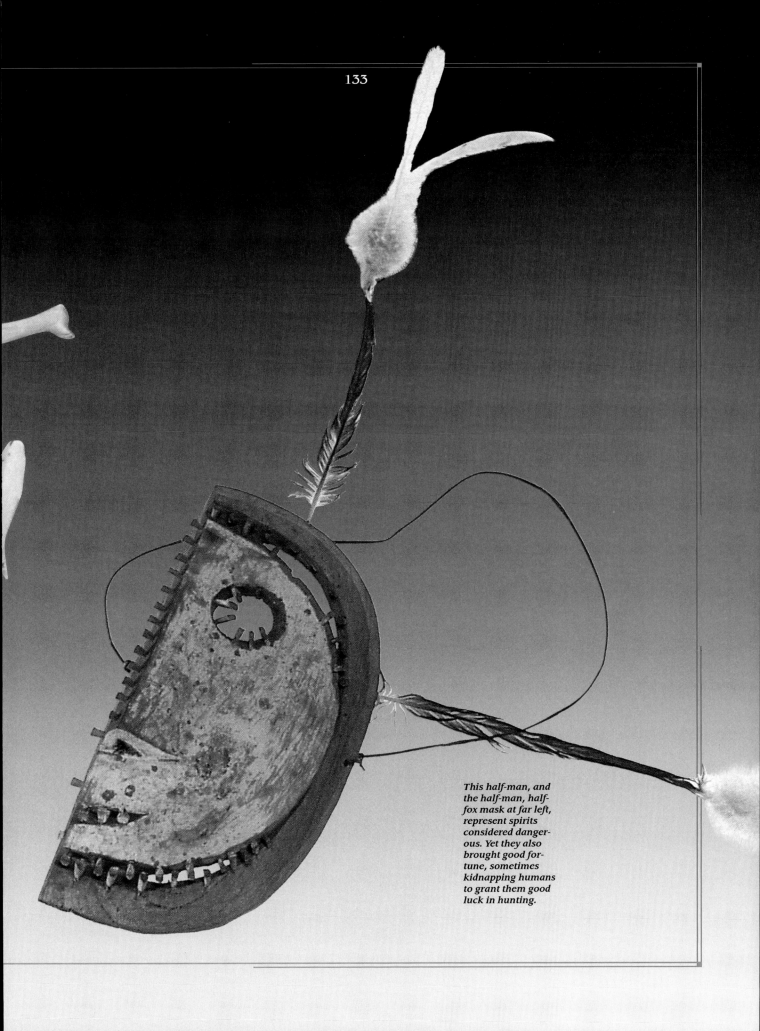

This half-man, and the half-man, half-fox mask at far left, represent spirits considered dangerous. Yet they also brought good fortune, sometimes kidnapping humans to grant them good luck in hunting.

SHAPES OF SPIRIT CREATURES

The hinged door on an otter spirit mask opens to reveal the spirit's human face, something all inuas possessed. The two bentwood hoops symbolize the otter's universe.

A grizzly bear spirit mask dangles beneath its jaw a salmon—its principal food. The hoops and swan feathers probably mark the extent of the bear spirit's realm.

The human face of a seabird's inua peers out from the creature's open beak. In many Eskimo tales, animals pushed open their mouths in order to change into a person.

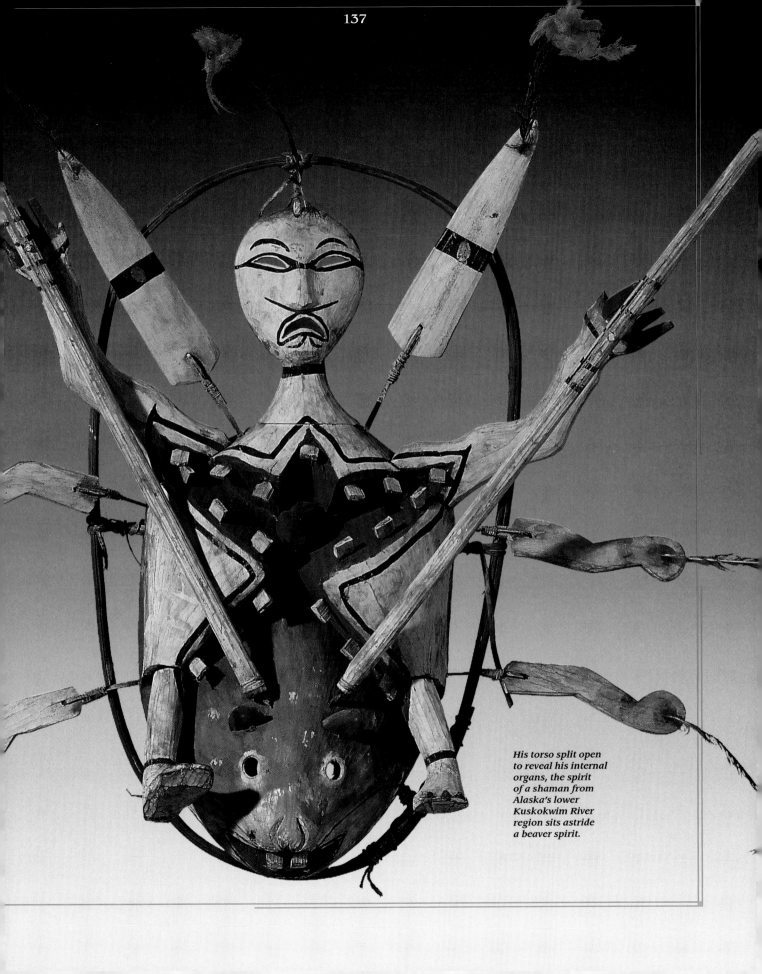

His torso split open to reveal his internal organs, the spirit of a shaman from Alaska's lower Kuskokwim River region sits astride a beaver spirit.

3

A STRUGGLE TO PRESERVE TRADITION

British explorers John Ross and William Edward Parry trade metal knives for narwhal tusks during the historic first encounter between Europeans and Polar Eskimos, near Greenland's Cape York in 1818. The drawing for this lithograph was done by Hans Zakaeus, an Inuit from southern Greenland who served as the expedition's interpreter.

More than 1,000 years ago, two resourceful peoples were embarked on journeys that would bring them into competition for a seemingly unlikely prize—the desolate expanse known later as Greenland. Lying largely within the Arctic Circle, the island was dominated by a massive icecap that shielded much of the interior, leaving only the rocky perimeter habitable. Even there at the fringes, none but the hardiest souls could hope to endure and prosper. Yet the two groups destined for Greenland were no strangers to the rigors of the Far North. Approaching slowly from the west in a migration that spanned centuries were Eskimos of what would later be called the Thule culture—fur-clad hunters who were drifting ever farther from their ancestral base in Alaska as their main quarry, the bowhead whale, extended its range. Advancing swiftly from the east were Norse colonists who set sail from Viking settlements on Iceland. Those far-ranging Scandinavians were legendary for their toughness and tenacity. But it was the Eskimos who would prevail against the fierce elements and the forbidding Norsemen to make Greenland their own.

The Norse colonists reached Greenland long before their would-be rivals. In the year 986, an expedition led by Erik the Red, a man whose temper matched his fiery red beard, touched down on the island's rugged but verdant southwestern coast. His followers arrived in a flotilla of 14 square-sailed ships. On board were some 400 people, along with cattle and sheep to provide them with meat, hide, and wool. Erik had first explored this coast a few years earlier, after being temporarily banished from Iceland for his involvement in murderous feuds. A promoter as well as an adventurer, he dubbed the place Greenland for the sensible reason that "men will be more readily persuaded to go there if the land has an attractive name." The colonists he enticed to Greenland established two villages there. One, called the Eastern Settlement, was located near the southern tip of the island. The other, known as the Western Settlement, lay some 300 miles up the west coast, near the modern-day capital of Godthaab.

In an earlier epoch, Greenland had been home to Eskimos of the so-called Dorset culture, which mysteriously disappeared some time about 100 BC. Erik's colonists found intriguing relics of their existence, including tools and fragments of skin boats. But centuries would pass before the Norse settlers met with Eskimos in the flesh. By then the Greenland communities were thriving. The Western Settlement alone contained nearly 300 homesteads along with a score of churches and a convent and monastery, where colonists practiced their adopted faith of Christianity. At its peak, the community contained as many as 5,000 residents. They seemed to be strong enough to withstand any challenge. But sometime in the 12th century, the Thule migrants crossed Smith Sound from Ellesmere Island, plying open waters in kayaks and umiaks and traversing ice and snow by dogsled. Norsemen from the Western Settlement—who were avid hunters as well as herdsmen—probably first encountered the Eskimos about the year 1250 while sailing up the coast in pursuit of polar bears and whales. The colonists dismissed the short, dark-skinned strangers as Skraellings, or "barbarians." According to a Norse account: "Hunters have found some little people whom they call Skraellings. They have no iron at all; they use missiles made of walrus tusk and sharp stones for knives."

The first encounters between the two sides were evidently peaceful. As the Eskimos ventured farther south in search of prey, however, they began to compete with Norse hunters for sea mammals. Tolerance gave way to suspicion and resentment, culminating in bloody confrontations. Both Eskimo legends and Norse written accounts tell of a deepening conflict. About 1350 Eskimo attacks forced residents in the Western Settlement to abandon their homes so abruptly that they left behind their cattle and sheep. Having gained control of that region, the Eskimos pushed on to the south and launched assaults against the Eastern Settlement. In 1379 one Norse account reported an Eskimo attack that killed 18 men. By 1500 the Norse homesteads lay in ruins. Icelanders who visited Greenland in the early 1500s found only Eskimos living there.

Eskimo hostility was only partly responsible for the collapse of the settlements. The Norse economy depended on maritime trade, and that commerce declined for various reasons. For one thing, European demand for hides and other goods from Greenland decreased in the face of competition from Russian trading companies. At the same time, the Eskimos as they pushed southward may have depleted the game sought by Norse hunters. To make matters worse for the settlers, the climate turned colder during the 14th and 15th centuries. Plummeting temperatures disrupted

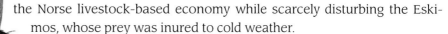

Dozens of amulets, including a loon's foot for kayaking, a tern's head for fishing, and a seal's claw to build strong arms, dangle from a Netsilik boy's parka brought back from the Arctic by explorer Knud Rasmussen. Worn by Inuits of all ages to gain spiritual power, the charms were considered especially helpful to children.

the Norse livestock-based economy while scarcely disturbing the Eskimos, whose prey was inured to cold weather.

Whatever the causes of the Norse extinction, the result was singular. For once, people native to the New World were victors rather than victims in a confrontation with Europeans. The Eskimos prevailed, and their traditions persisted. But this would not always be the case in the centuries to come. Across the icy realm extending for more than 3,000 miles from Alaska to Greenland, a succession of explorers, whalers, traders, missionaries, and officials would have a profound impact on the Eskimos and their environment. By the 20th century, indigenous peoples who had long endured some of the harshest conditions on earth would find themselves besieged by outside forces that threatened the very survival of their culture.

Less than a century after the Norse disappeared from Greenland, Eskimos on the North American continent encountered Europeans of a different ilk. Unlike the colonists in Greenland, these intruders had no intention of settling down but came searching for the fabled Northwest Passage—a proposed shortcut to the riches of Asia that had mesmerized voyagers since the time of Christopher Columbus. It became such an obsession that explorers would hunt for that passage for more than four centuries, stumbling in the process on more than a dozen Eskimo groups along the shores of Greenland and Canada.

The first such European adventurer to record his encounter with Eskimos was Martin Frobisher, who sailed westward in 1576. A dour 41-year-old Englishman, Frobisher had honed his seaman's skills as a pirate. With a crew of 18 on a little three-masted vessel named *Gabriel,* he skirted the southern tip of Greenland and headed northwest, struggling through storms and treacherous pack ice until he entered a broad inlet that he took to be the long-sought Passage to Cathay. Had he continued farther, he would have discovered that the inlet was simply a large bay on the southeastern coast of Baffin Island.

Near the mouth of Frobisher Bay, as it was known thereafter, the English commander spotted an approaching flotilla of Eskimos in kayaks. Invited aboard the *Gabriel* to trade, the Eskimos were friendly at first. In the days that followed, however, they showed flashes of hostility, a sign that they might have been mistreated by earlier European visitors. Perhaps to forestall any problems with Frobisher, they took five of his men captive after the sailors went ashore. Frobisher, seeking a hostage to bargain for their release, lured a kayaker to the side of the ship by ringing a bell. Then, according to one witness, he demonstrated his prodigious strength by plucking "both the man and his light boat out of the sea." When the Eskimos later retreated to the interior of Baffin Island, presumably with their five captives, Frobisher sailed for London with his own hostage. Like other natives of the New World hauled off to Europe by early explorers, the Eskimo soon fell ill and died.

In addition to his captive, Frobisher brought back a heavy chunk of stone that was thought to contain gold. In 1577 he set sail once more for Baffin Island, determined to gain riches there if he could not find a way to the Orient. Shortly after arriving, he captured some Eskimos in the hope of exchanging them for the five sailors seized on the previous expedition. Skirmishes broke out between the local people and Frobisher's crew. In one encounter, several Eskimos flung themselves off a cliff into the sea rather than be taken captive. "They supposed us to be eaters of man's flesh," wrote one of the crew members. The sailors harbored fears of their own about the Eskimos. Believing that one wizened old woman they had taken prisoner was a witch, some of Frobisher's men forced her to take off her boots "to see if she were cloven footed," a crewman reported. To their surprise, her feet turned out to be normal.

Frobisher's flotilla carried home a cargo of 200 tons of rock similar to the first promising sample as well as three kidnapped Eskimos—a man, a woman, and her child. Despite written accounts from the Frobisher expedition depicting Eskimos as primitives who ate only raw meat and used "neither table, stoole, or table cloth," the three were so dignified and respectful when they were presented to Queen Elizabeth that she granted the man a special favor: permission to launch his kayak on the Thames and hunt swans. The Eskimo did not have long to enjoy the privilege, however. He and his two companions contracted pneumonia and died within a month or two after their arrival.

Frobisher made one more expedition to Baffin Island in 1578, but like the earlier voyages, it yielded him no fortune: The rocks he retrieved contained nothing more than iron pyrites, or fool's gold. The fate of his missing five crewmen would remain a mystery for nearly three centuries. Then, in 1862, an old Eskimo woman named Ookijoxy Ninoo told American explorer Charles Hall a story from the oral tradition that was later substantiated by archaeological evidence. After the departure of Frobisher's third and final expedition, the Eskimos had freed the five Englishmen.

THE LOST PEOPLE

Starting with the earliest arctic voyages, European and American explorers carried Inuits back with them along with more traditional specimens of flora and fauna. Although some Inuits were kidnapped, most came voluntarily, lured by curiosity and promises of a speedy return and gifts of valuable tools and weapons. Their fate was usually tragic, most of them succumbing to disease. The last to be uprooted were six Polar Eskimos brought to New York City in 1897 by Robert Peary. Within months, five of them died of pneumonia, leaving only a seven-year-old boy named Minik *(below),* who was adopted by the superintendent of the American Museum of Natural History.

A colored handbill printed in Nuremberg, Germany, in 1567 advertises the public display of an Inuit mother and child who were taken from Labrador by French sailors.

Minik models his fur parka and trousers shortly after his arrival in New York City in 1897. Twelve years later, he returned to Greenland, relearned his native language, and served as an interpreter for an American expedition to the Axel Heiberg Island region. Minik died of influenza in 1918 while he was working as a lumberjack in New Hampshire.

They fled to Kodlunarn Island, where Frobisher's crew had been digging ore. There they built a boat from some timbers left behind and sailed off, only to perish in the arctic cold.

In 1585 another English mariner seeking the Northwest Passage, John Davis, managed to initiate friendlier relations with the native peoples. Davis's journey took him to a Greenland fjord not far from the old Western Settlement. He brought with him a four-man orchestra expressly to entertain the Eskimos. Once ashore, the musicians played and the sailors danced, luring an appreciative audience who arrived in kayaks. One friendly Eskimo greeted a member of Davis's crew with a kiss on the hand, a gesture undoubtedly acquired through earlier contact with Europeans. On a later voyage, his crewmen engaged in good-natured wrestling matches with the Greenlanders. "We found them strong and nimble," wrote Davis, "for they cast some of our men that were good wrestlers."

Davis found the locals eager to trade their clothing, kayaks, sealskins, and fish. As other explorers would confirm, what they wanted most in return was iron, which they found far more suitable than ivory or bone for tools and weapons. Their desire for iron was so keen that Davis found the Eskimos "marvellous theevish." They carried off everything of iron that was not strapped down and even chopped through cables to make off with a ship's anchor. Davis was at first amused by their boldness, but finally ordered that a cannon be fired to frighten them away.

For all of John Davis's efforts to humor the Eskimos, his expeditions to Greenland and beyond were marred by two lethal incidents. He lost two crewmen to an Eskimo attack along the coast of Labrador, and a dispute in southern Greenland over the quality of a kayak offered in trade led to the death of three Eskimos. As the Norse colonists had learned to their dismay, the Eskimos, once antagonized, made determined foes. When intruders committed outrages against them such as hauling off captives, they heeded the lesson and often lashed out at the next party of white men who came along. And some Eskimo bands living in isolation looked with suspicion on all strangers and needed little provocation to attack them.

Such was the fate of the crew that accompanied the celebrated English mariner Henry Hudson on his search for the Northwest Passage aboard the vessel *Discovery* in 1610. After sailing up the strait between Baffin Island and the North American mainland and entering the great bay that would bear his name, Hudson and his crew spent an arduous winter trapped in the ice. The following summer, angered by a reduction in their already short rations, the crew of the *Discovery* mutinied and cast Hudson and eight others adrift in a tiny boat, never to be seen again. Fate then turned against the mutineers when they approached an inhabited island at the entrance to the bay. After a day of barter with the local people, they let down their guard and went ashore unarmed. For unknown reasons, the Eskimos turned on them with knife and arrow, killing four of them. The remaining mutineers fled back to their ship and set sail for England.

Hudson's failure to find the Northwest Passage did not deter other explorers from following in his tracks. Hudson Bay proved to be a dead end for mariners seeking a route to the Orient, but it did offer merchant ships access to the fur-rich interior of North America. In 1670 the Hudson's Bay Company received a royal charter from England's King Charles II to inaugurate a fur-trading enterprise. At the lower end of Hudson Bay, the company established a post called Fort Churchill, which became a base for trading ventures and for further efforts to find a way to the Pacific. In one such attempt, launched in 1770, a young Scotsman named Samuel Hearne set out overland from Fort Churchill with an escort of Chipewyan Indians. Hearne and his Indian escorts trekked northwestward for hundreds of miles before they reached the Coppermine River, which they followed north all the way to the Arctic Ocean. There, near the river's ice-choked mouth, they encountered a band of Eskimos. The meeting was unfortunate, for there had long been bad blood between Eskimos and the subarctic tribes. On this occasion, the Chipewyans took the offensive, slaughtering the Eskimos without provocation.

The route Hearne and his escorts explored was not navigable, and the search for the Northwest Passage continued, with far-reaching effects on Eskimos. In 1821 English explorers William Edward Parry and George Lyon tried to find the passage by skirting the entrance to Hudson Bay and entering Foxe Basin to the north. But at the far end of that basin, their ships became trapped in the ice for two successive winters. Fortunately for the stranded explorers, they met with hospitable Iglulik Eskimos. The well-provisioned Englishmen befriended the Iglulik and offered them food when the seal hunting was bad, picked up their Inuit dialect, and mastered some of their customs and crafts, such as building snowhouses and making dogsleds. Lyon visited the Iglulik and invited the shaman Tollemak to come aboard his ship to cure one of his sick officers. Lyon went so far as to submit to the painful tattooing that adorned the local women. Overlooking the occasional theft of iron or wood, which the Iglulik lacked and coveted, Lyon praised their character: "I verily believe that there does not exist a more honest set of people than the tribe with whom we had so long

an acquaintance." After Parry and Lyon returned to England in 1823, their appreciative accounts brought the Iglulik to the notice of the world.

Parry had already helped bring to light another group, the Polar Eskimos, who would figure prominently in future expeditions. The world's northernmost population, they lived along Smith Sound on a narrow stretch of the Greenland coast bounded on three sides by immense glaciers. Parry had encountered them in 1818 while serving on an expedition led by Scotsman John Ross. "They exist in a corner of the world by far the most secluded which has yet been discovered," wrote Ross, who spoke with the Polar Eskimos through his interpreter, John Sackhouse, an Inuit from southern Greenland. "Until the moment of our arrival," Ross added, they "believed themselves to be the only inhabitants of the universe, and that all the rest of the world was a mass of ice."

Ross went on to experiment with steam propulsion in the Arctic—his paddleboat became icebound in 1829 off Canada's Boothia Peninsula for three years, and only the aid of the Netsilik Eskimos there kept the crew alive. In the interim, the Polar Eskimos were left alone to pursue their unique way of life. They numbered only about 200 persons in several small, widely scattered villages, and they possessed limited technology. Standard Eskimo equipment such as the bow and arrow, the umiak, and the kayak had been lost to their culture under extreme conditions that restricted the range of their subsistence activities. They did not fish or hunt sea mammals in open water—the ocean was frozen for all but about four weeks a year—and depended almost entirely on harpooning seals, walruses, and polar bears on the pack ice.

The Polar Eskimos once again became the focus of attention in the

Members of an Inuit camp on Boothia Peninsula leave their igloos to greet two British naval officers in a watercolor painted by Captain John Ross during his 1829 expedition. The villagers, Ross reported, "were delighted with the representation; each recognising his own house."

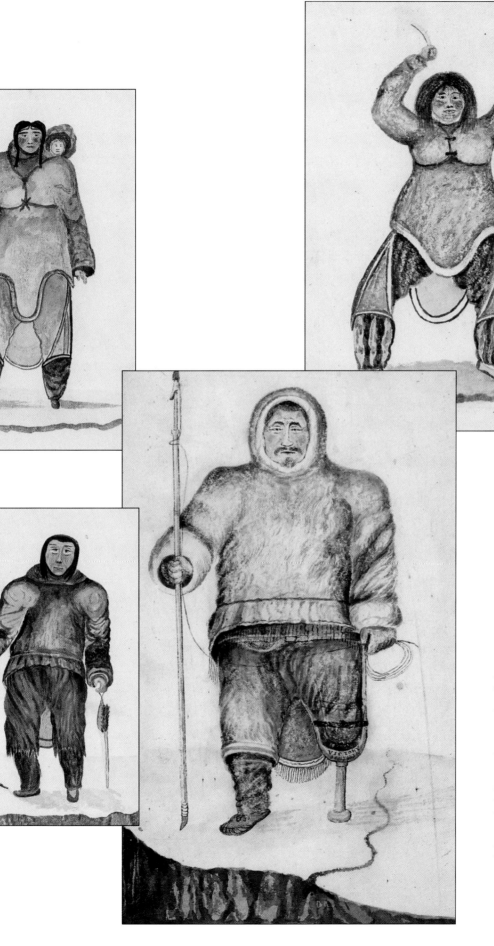

Ross's watercolors provide a rare glimpse of early-19th-century Inuit life. The explorer dispensed presents to win the peoples' trust. The hunter at left, having lost a leg to a polar bear, wears a wooden limb provided by the ship's carpenter—a gift, Ross reported, that made the man "serviceable once more to himself and his community."

mid-1800s during the protracted search for British explorer John Franklin, whose two-ship expedition, mounted in 1845, vanished while searching for the Northwest Passage. The two vessels, it turned out, had become trapped in a perennial ice jam off King William Island, west of the Boothia Peninsula. Franklin and the 129 men who manned his ships all perished of scurvy and famine. But their fate remained a mystery to the outside world until 1859. Before then, nearly 40 separate rescue missions were initiated in search of the lost mariners. One such effort was launched from the United States in May 1853 under the command of a Philadelphia physician and adventurer named Elisha Kent Kane. After his previous excursion to hunt for Franklin a few years earlier, Kane was convinced that the Franklin expedition had headed north through Smith Sound, and he probed in that direction. Later that year, his own little brig, *Advance,* was stranded amid the ice in Smith Sound, and he and his crew had to winter over. They were still trapped when they met the Polar Eskimos in the spring.

Among those who approached Kane's vessel in the spring of 1854 was Metek, a tall, sturdily built man who wore striking boots made from the lower part of a polar bear's legs with soles and claws intact. Metek and his seven companions lived some 70 miles to the south in Etah, the world's northernmost permanent settlement. Kane bartered with his visitors, swapping barrel staves, beads, and needles for four sled dogs and walrus meat while tactfully ignoring the stolen goods the Eskimos carried back to their sleds. In the autumn, with the ship still icebound and Kane and his crew facing the grim prospect of a second winter in Smith Sound, Metek's people went too far. They pilfered a pair of buffalo robes and made off with Kane's best dog and cooking utensils. Kane caught some of the thieves, including Metek's wife, and held them hostage. Metek showed up several days later with a sled laden with stolen goods. After these were handed over to Kane, the two men negotiated a kind of treaty of mutual aid. The Etah people would stop stealing and would bring fresh meat to trade when it was available, sell or lend the white men dogs, and show them where to hunt. Kane pledged in return not to harm the Eskimos and to give them presents, invite them aboard ship, and join them on hunts.

That both sides generally abided by the pact was a testament to good faith and to the skillful mediation of Hans Hendrik, a young Eskimo belonging to Kane's party. He had been recruited at the age of 18 in southern Greenland. But his early years in an Eskimo community there still had not prepared him for the challenges of life so far north, especially the interminable darkness of winter. "Never had I seen the dark season like this," he said later. "I thought we should have no daylight anymore. I was seized with fright." But Hendrik conquered his fear and proved to be instrumental in the survival of Kane and his men. He served as interpreter during discussions with the Polar Eskimos and hunted seals for the starving crew.

After a second icebound winter, Kane and his men linked up with a Danish ship in the spring of 1855 and left Arctic waters—but without their Eskimo companion. Hendrik had left the ship just weeks before, walking to a community south of Etah to get walrus hide for boot soles. He found a compelling reason to stay there: He married a local girl who had cared for him when he had fallen ill during a trip to Etah the previous winter.

Some years later, Hendrik was recruited from his remote refuge to serve in the first of three additional arctic expeditions he would undertake. One of these adventures left him marooned on the ice along with his wife and four children and a dozen other Eskimos and white crewmen. While the ice floe drifted 1,500 miles over a period of nearly six months, Hendrik and his companions stayed alive by killing seals until they were rescued off southern Labrador.

Although such forays brought a measure of fame to Hendrik and other Eskimos who played a part, the explorations augured ill for the inhabitants of the Far North as a whole. Once paths were charted through Arctic waters, the Eskimos risked losing the isolation that up until that time had shielded them from the waves of disease and disruption that were ravaging native peoples elsewhere. In remote areas of Greenland and other sites along the North Atlantic, the consequences were just being felt. To the west, along the Pacific shores of the Aleutian Islands and the Alaska Peninsula, however, the onslaught was well under way.

The 15,000 or so Aleuts who lived along the Pacific endured a much harsher introduction to European ways at the hands of Russian fur traders. Seeing benefits for themselves, the Aleuts were at first eager to trade but would soon discover that these outsiders had come not to exchange goods equitably with the local people but to exploit them. For the first time, natives of the Far North had to bow to the demands of Europeans. The Russians were attracted to the New World in the 18th century by the prospect of expanding their already lucrative Siberian fur trade. In the summer of 1741, Danish-born explorer Vitus Bering—who had earlier navigated the Bering Strait and reconnoitered the Bering Sea for the Russians—was returning from an exploratory voyage along the southern

THE MESSENGER FEAST

As darkness and frigid temperatures tightened their grip on Alaska's North Slope in the winter of 1988, more than 2,000 Inupiat traveled to Barrow to bask in the spiritual light and warmth of the Messenger Feast, or Kivgiq, a festival that had not been held in some 70 years. Crammed into the tiny gymnasium of Ipalook Elementary School, the celebrants sang, danced, and exchanged gifts for three days. All the while, a musician pounded a large, wooden, box-shaped drum, filling the air with a resonant, rhythmic pulsation.

Once the main social event of the North Slope, Kivgiq traditionally involved an exchange of gifts between a host village, which sponsored the event, and a guest village. The primary purpose of the feast, whose name is derived from the messengers who delivered the invitations, was to enable people to obtain goods unavailable in their region. A village in an area where caribou were abundant, for example, would present caribou meat to people who lived where the animals were scarce. Kivgiq also enhanced the social status of the hosts, whose gifts were more elaborate than those of their guests, and renewed the ties of friendship between the two communities.

In legend, the feast was bestowed upon the Inupiat by a sacred eagle in ancient times. But about 1915, Christian missionaries deemed the festival immoral and banned it. Inupiat leaders revived Kivgiq in order to bolster traditional culture, which was being eroded by drug addiction, alcoholism, and other modern problems. Some details of the event have changed. Messengers still participate, for example, but their role is symbolic because communities now use fax machines and telephones to organize the event. Nevertheless, the spirit of sharing prevails. The Inupiat of Barrow open their homes to visitors from other towns and prepare banquets featuring such traditional foods as duck, geese, whale meat and blubber, fish, and caribou. At Kivgiq itself, individuals as well as communities renew the bonds of friendship by presenting gifts to one another. Between presentations, dance troupes from various villages perform, amicably competing to see who can best mimic the motions of birds and other animals.

Ever since 1988, attendance at the annual event has mushroomed. The mayor of the North Slope Borough suggested a reason for the feast's popularity. "We can enjoy Western entertainment, yet it falls short," he explained. "There is a social and spiritual need inside us as Inupiat which can only be satisfied by our own traditions."

Kivgiq invitations were at one time delivered by messengers carrying sticks such as the one at left. Tufts of wolverine fur symbolize the gifts guests were expected to bring. At right, Thomas Itta, Sr., carries a messenger stick at a modern feast.

Singers and drummers from Wainwright, Alaska, perform at Kivgiq. While the men pound the rims of their drums to keep time for dancers, the women sing and sway gently to the music while waving feathered wands.

Jakey Kunuk of Point Hope, Alaska, uses exaggerated gestures to tell a hunting tale. Called motion dancing, this traditional form of storytelling relies not upon words but rather upon music and pantomime.

A group from Wainwright proudly presents a polar bear skin to the people of Anaktuvuk Pass in the Brooks Range, a region where polar bears are scarce. Among the gifts exchanged by the two communities were knives, rifles, whaling equipment, and cassette players.

A delighted Zacharias Hugo of Anaktuvuk Pass (left) accepts a walrus skull and attached tusks from Alaq, a skilled hunter from Wainwright, Alaska.

coast of Alaska when he was shipwrecked on an island west of the Aleutians. Although Bering and most of his men died of scurvy, a handful survived by eating the flesh of sea otters. When they returned to Siberia after rebuilding their boat, the rich, dark otter pelts they brought with them triggered a rush of fortune-hunting fur traders to the newly charted waters.

As the Russian traders pushed eastward, the Aleuts sustained blow after blow. Small parties of Russians armed with muskets and even cannon took one island after another by storm and subdued the Aleuts, forcing the men to use their superb hunting skills to pursue the sea otter and other quarry by threatening the Aleuts bodily or holding their women and children hostage. The Russians paid for some of the furs with beads, hatchets, and other trade goods, but they seized the rest as tax, claiming that the Aleuts were now subjects of imperial Russia. Aleuts who resisted were ruthlessly suppressed. By 1766 the Aleut population had been reduced by more than two-thirds as a result of violence, privation, and disease.

To the east, on Kodiak Island, the 3,500 or so native inhabitants known as Koniags repulsed Russian traders repeatedly before being defeated and forced to accept the first permanent foreign settlement on their soil in 1784. The sponsor of this colony, a firm that came to be known as the Russian-American Company, inaugurated schools and Russian Orthodox churches for the islanders in the hope of making them more tractable. In the years to come, the company forcibly recruited men in order to extend its reach along the coast of Alaska. Every year company agents pressed into service several thousand males from Kodiak Island and surrounding areas. Some were used as warriors. In 1799, for example, the company deployed native fighting men in a fleet of 550 kayaks to discourage the Tlingit Indians from interfering with the founding of a post at Sitka. Other men served under duress as hunters of sea otters and other furbearing animals on lengthy expeditions that ranged as far south as California. The absence of males condemned Koniag villages to food shortages. Famine combined with diseases contracted from the Russians and the losses suffered during sporadic rebellions decimated the native society. By 1805 the population of Kodiak Island was half of what it had been 20 years earlier when the Russians first arrived.

By the early 19th century, the supply of otters and seals was dwindling along the coast because of overhunting, and the Russian-American Company sent explorers into the interior of southwest Alaska. The goal was to locate new sources of furs, in particular beaver pelts, and to extend the territorial claims of the imperial government, which now played a larger

A hunter sprawls on the sea ice off Cape Celveland in northwestern Greenland to drink from a melt pool. In spring, the saline in the ice sinks, leaving the upper layer relatively fresh. When the meltwater is too far away to reach with the mouth or is covered by thin ice, the Inuit use straws made of hollow bone, like the two shown above.

role in managing the company. By 1833 the Russians had made contact with several groups of Eskimos and established trading posts along three major rivers, the Nushagak, the Kuskokwim, and the Yukon.

Relations between the inhabitants of the interior and the Russian newcomers were relatively civil, thanks in part to efforts by the Russian government to control the earlier abuses that had so antagonized the Aleuts and Koniags. In time, the government even prohibited the company from establishing a trading post without first obtaining the permission of the local populace. The Russian traders were also restrained by the fact that they were more isolated and vulnerable to attack in the interior than along the coast. They came to rely on persuasion rather than coercion in winning over the Eskimos. Company agents sought to ingratiate themselves with men of influence, who in turn would encourage their fellow hunters to supply the traders with furs. As payment, the leaders would receive money and goods such as combs, jewelry, knives, and needles to distribute to their comrades.

This largely peaceful exchange was disrupted when a smallpox epidemic ravaged the interior from 1838 into 1839, killing up to two-thirds of the residents of some communities. Seeing that the Russian traders were unscathed by the disease—they alone had been vaccinated—the Eskimos assumed the intruders were using evil medicine to destroy them. They attacked a Russian trading post, killing the employees and seizing furs.

Meanwhile, the Eskimos continued to trade with their traditional partners. For centuries, Eskimos of western Alaska had carried on a thriving interchange across the Bering Strait with the native Chukchi of Siberia. Annual trade fairs had been held on both sides of the strait. By the early 19th century, the Chukchi were supplying the Alaskan Eskimos with reindeer hides and Russian tobacco, which the Eskimos avidly smoked, chewed, or snuffed through bird-bone tubes. In return, the Chukchi received furs, skins, walrus tusks, and whalebone. Alarmed by such competition, the Russian-American Company sent a small expedition deep into the Alaskan interior in 1842 to establish ties with Eskimos there. Leading the foray was Lieutenant Lavrentiy Zagoskin, an adventurous naval officer. For roughly two years, he and his half-dozen companions traveled by snowshoe in winter and skin canoe in summer, covering more than 3,000 miles along the Yukon and Kuskokwim Rivers. He compiled hundreds of pages on the lives of the Eskimos he met, leaving a treasure-trove of material for future historians and anthropologists. But his efforts to change the trading habits of the upriver Eskimos went for naught, and their net-

An Inupiat girl bounces joyously during the Naluktaq, or Blanket Toss, that caps the festival held in north Alaskan villages to celebrate a successful whaling season. Villagers jump according to rank, with the whaling captains going first, the harpooners second, and the wives of the whaling captains third—followed by the rest of the community.

work of commerce with their Siberian counterparts continued to thrive.

Beginning in the mid-19th century, Russians had to contend with another competitor in the struggle for Alaska's resources, the United States. In 1848 American ships began to exploit the rich whaling waters north of the Bering Strait. For more than 50 years to come, hundreds of whaling ships would sail from San Francisco harbor each summer to prowl the waters off the north coast of Alaska and of Canada's Yukon. This trend continued unabated after the United States purchased Alaska from the Russians in 1867. The main draw was the bowhead whale, which was in demand not only for its oil—a source of soap, lubricants, and candles—but also for its whalebone, or baleen. Those long, flexible strips, used by the whale to strain its food from the water, were prized for a wide range of manufactured products, from corset stays, buttons, and skirt hoops to fishing rods and riding crops.

At first the residents of Point Hope and other Eskimo settlements saw little of the ships, which put in to shore only for supplies or to seek refuge from storms. But the price of baleen was soaring—between 1850 and 1880, it jumped sixfold to $2.00 a pound—and the ship captains soon discovered that they could augment their haul by buying the whalebone from Eskimo hunters. To pay for the baleen and for precious walrus ivory, the captains crammed their ships with steel knives and tobacco and with two potentially destructive items that were commonly offered to native peoples in defiance of American law—firearms and liquor.

The coastal peoples welcomed the seasonal trade initially, but after 1880 they began to feel increasingly pressured. Introduction of the steam-powered whaling vessel that year meant that ships could break through ice before the summer thaw. As much as one-fourth of the whaling fleet wintered over in order to be ready to work when the ice was thin enough for the steamers to make headway in the spring. During the 1880s, some whaling companies even set up permanent stations along the coast. The American whaling industry thus became a year-round influence as Eskimo men were hired to work on the ships and to operate smaller boats from the dozen or so whaling stations. As payment, the Eskimos usually received flour, crackers, molasses, and other trade goods.

In 1905 the price for baleen peaked at $4.90 a pound, only to plunge thereafter as other materials began to replace it. The sharp drop in price, combined with the severe depletion of the whale population as a result of overhunting, brought American commercial whaling in the Arctic Ocean nearly to an end by 1910. Native hunters now found few whales in their ancestral waters, and the flow of trade goods many Eskimos had come to rely on was greatly reduced. The collapse of the baleen trade put further stress on a population that had already been decimated by smallpox, measles, influenza, venereal disease, and other ills introduced by the whalers. Only 120 or so of the 2,000 Eskimos in the Mackenzie River delta region survived the whaling heyday.

Along with imported diseases, alcohol contributed to precipitous population declines. A fearful example of the harm alcohol could do to native peoples occurred in 1878, when several American whaling ships heading home after the summer season stopped south of the Bering Strait at Saint

Enclosed by a whale-bone fence, a graveyard at Point Hope, Alaska, honors the dead with both Christian headstones and traditional Inupiat grave markers. The tallest markers are jawbones of bowhead whales, placed over the final resting places of whaling captains in order to affirm the community's abiding link with these mighty sea creatures.

Lawrence Island to trade liquor for baleen. Many of the island's 1,500 inhabitants then fell into such a drunken debauch that they could not take part in the annual walrus hunt. Those who did venture out to hunt were hindered by bad weather, and famine ensued. By the following summer, 1,000 islanders lay dead. The loss of population was never recouped. Naturalist John Muir, visiting the island in 1880 aboard an American ship investigating reports of mass deaths, observed entire settlements devoid of life and littered with bleached bones.

Whaling was not the only industry to have a destructive impact on the native way of life. When white entrepreneurs built six salmon canneries on Kodiak Island during the 1880s, they claimed the harvest from streams that had been the mainstay of local fishermen and their families. People who had once subsisted on what they caught themselves came to rely instead on wages paid by the canneries. When work was scarce or wages dropped, the islanders suffered. Similarly, when thousands of white fortune hunters swarmed through the Yukon River region after the discovery of gold there in the late 1890s, some Eskimos managed to find work in the mining camps. But by 1920, the gold rush had ended, leaving Eskimos who had grown dependent on wages to fend for themselves.

Such disruption spread far beyond Alaska and the Yukon. By the early 20th century, Eskimos clear across the Arctic were undergoing rapid transformations in their way of life. An important agent of change in many areas was the fur trade, which expanded as demand increased for the Arctic fox pelts and other exotic furs of the Far North. During the 1920s, the Hudson's Bay Company opened more than a dozen trading posts in the Canadian Arctic, and other companies established rival posts. After World War I, Arctic fox pelts were so prized that an Eskimo could support himself and his family solely on the income earned by trapping the animals and selling their skins. A single such pelt fetched $40 on average, and an especially fine one could bring in as much as $70. By trapping 300 or so foxes, an Eskimo could earn up to $18,000 a year. But as with the baleen trade, the heyday was brief and the aftermath disheartening. During the Great Depression, the demand for pelts declined, and Eskimos were left with little income and a severely depleted population of furbearing species.

Regular contact with outsiders transformed not only the culture of the Eskimos but also their economy. New tools and weapons supplemented or even replaced the simple and elegant technology of old. Eskimos coveted the manufactured implements newly available to them for the rewards they brought. Firearms, for example, killed more game faster than arrows and spears. And harpoon heads that were made from brass or other metals proved tougher than those made of bone.

Every new tool or material the Eskimos adopted increased their dependence on outsiders. To be nearer the sources of jobs and trade goods, some groups abandoned their seminomadic way of life, settling near trading posts, mining camps, and whaling stations. Others adhered to the traditional routine but acquired new weapons that came close to exhausting their old resources. With their high-powered rifles, the Copper Eskimos of Canada so reduced the caribou herds—by as much as 90 percent in a decade, according to one estimate—that they became largely reliant on traders for food and clothing as well as firearms and ammunition. Eskimos of the eastern Arctic, who formerly ate only meat and fish, bought flour to make bannock, a pan-baked bread introduced by Scottish whalers. Even the rigorous self-reliance of the Polar Eskimos was eroded after they helped the renowned American explorer Robert Peary reach the vicinity of the North Pole in 1909. Peary later bought virtually all of their traditional weapons and gear to display in American museums, and the Polar Eskimos thus had to rely in part on imported merchandise.

Like the whalers, gold seekers, and fur traders, missionaries of various faiths had a powerful impact on Eskimo culture. Beginning in 1721 with the founding of a Lutheran mission in Greenland, Christian outposts were established throughout the Far North. Although primarily concerned with conversions, the missionaries often looked after the worldly interests of their charges as well, learning their language and attempting to shield them from exploitation by other outsiders. In northern Labrador, Protestant missionaries of the Moravian faith even operated trading posts in an effort to keep the Eskimos away from such baleful influences as the liquor sold by white traders. Missionaries of sundry denominations also founded schools, cared for the sick, and buried the dead.

Even the most charitable efforts ran counter to Eskimo traditions, however. The medical care pro-

Blending Christian and Yupik beliefs, a Russian Orthodox priest blesses a cross carved in the ice during a ritual to bring a prosperous fishing season to the people of Napaskiak, Alaska.

Beneath a picture of Jesus playing with Inuit children, a Lutheran minister administers Holy Communion during a confirmation ceremony in Qaanaaq (Thule), Greenland. The youngsters are wearing their best clothes: the boys, pants made of polar bear fur; the girls, fox-fur knickers and thigh-length seal-skin boots.

vided at mission clinics, for example, saved lives but undermined the prestige of shamans. And missionaries antagonized many Eskimos when they attempted to suppress ancient rituals and customs. In Alaska, Moravians opposed the wearing of wooden spirit masks in dance festivals, and discouraged such ancestral practices as plural marriages and the temporary exchange of spouses.

No religious group showed greater respect for the prerogatives of indigenous peoples in the Far North than the missionaries of the Orthodox Church. After arriving on Kodiak Island in 1794, Russian Orthodox priests protested the economic exploitation of the Koniags and Aleuts and gained a large and loyal following among the local people. One lay worker by the name of Herman even built a refuge on Spruce Island in 1808 for Aleuts fleeing Russian oppression. (In 1970 he was canonized as Saint Herman, patron saint of Alaska and protector of native peoples.) Other factors strengthened the appeal of the Orthodox Church. Its rich ceremonies blended well with local festivals, and the church accepted members without requiring radical changes in their culture. Priests were instructed to conduct themselves among the native people as if they were guests in their home. The practice of recruiting and training Aleut and Eskimo clergy further heightened the indigenous feel of Orthodoxy. In time, churches with onion-shaped domes—some adorned with windows of seal intestines in place of stained glass—became a familiar sight not only on Kodiak Island and the Aleutians but also along the Alaska Peninsula and in parts of the interior.

Initially for other religious groups, establishing a rapport with indigenous peoples was often more difficult. A Moravian minister named John

Henry Kilbuck and his wife Edith arrived at Bethel on Alaska's Kuskokwim River in 1885, eager to teach and preach. A full-blooded Delaware Indian who had been raised on a Moravian mission in Kansas, John Kilbuck resembled the Eskimos in appearance and gradually came to identify with them. But his religious upbringing, like that of his wife, had steeped him in values far different from those of his hosts. At first, the Kilbucks were shocked by the premarital and extramarital sex practiced by the Eskimos. The killing of unwanted infants and the neglect of the dying seemed barbaric to the two missionaries, who were unaccustomed to the harsh realities of northern life. The Kilbucks insisted that converts adhere to Christian notions of propriety before being accepted as church members.

Inupiat men from Seward Peninsula tend reindeer harnessed to sleds. The animals were introduced to Alaska from Siberia in 1898 as part of an ill-conceived U.S. government plan to stimulate the local economy.

As time passed, however, the couple came to see the Eskimos and their traditions in a different light. They learned the local language, Yupik, participated in gift exchanges, and adopted an Eskimo child. They eventually became such an integral part of village life that residents referred to them and to the Eskimos living near their mission as the Kilbuchamuks, as if they were all native residents of the region. John Kilbuck developed especially close ties to the local people. He started a school and traveled to their widely scattered villages by dogsled to hold services and minister to the sick and the dying. In the process, he became increasingly sympathetic to native mores. His openness to the practice of spouse exchange eventually got him into trouble with his Moravian superiors. In 1898 he was dismissed from the ministry for having adulterous relations with an Eskimo woman and a female missionary at Bethel. He returned to the region a decade later as a teacher for the Bureau of Education and was welcomed by the villagers, who still admired and respected him.

Another missionary who made a deep impression on Alaska's Eski-

Sami brought to Alaska to teach reindeer-herding techniques stand in front of a tent in a sketch made by an Inupiat artist. Native Alaskans referred to the Sami as "card people" because their colorful outfits resembled the clothing worn by the king, queen, and jack in a deck of playing cards.

mos was Presbyterian Sheldon Jackson. Moved by the plight of native peoples who were languishing as contact with whites disrupted their traditional economy, he introduced the Eskimos to a new form of subsistence in 1891: reindeer herding. Jackson hoped that the meat and skins from the deer would help replace the shrinking whale harvests. Over the next decade, at first with private funds and then with government backing, Jackson imported 1,280 reindeer from Siberia. The animals were sent to missions so that local people could be schooled in the art of herding. To supervise the training of apprentices, Jackson brought in Chukchi Eskimos. When that did not work out, he recruited Laplanders, or Sami: indigenous herders from northern Norway.

Although the reindeer proliferated, interest among Eskimos in herding them gradually flagged. The herd of 50 or so animals given the apprentice after his training was too small to support a family. If he had to go on hunting, fishing, or trapping to live, then he had to either hire someone to tend the herd or neglect it and let the animals romp in the wild, where wolves preyed on them and the survivors often ran off to mingle with their cousins, the caribou. Herding also meant keeping on the move for most of the year to search out good grazing. These difficulties were compounded by conflict with the Sami, expert herders

La Plahderscamp.

who considered the local people inferior and increased their own holdings at Eskimo expense. During the 1930s, before the industry went into decline, several hundred thousand reindeer roamed the Alaska Range, but most were owned by Sami or by large white-dominated companies.

The process of change was accelerated by military forces during World War II. The eastern Arctic lay directly in the path of the shortest air routes between North America and Europe, and Eskimos found jobs building the airstrips, radio and weather stations, and barracks required by the Allies. In the process, shantytowns sprang up around military installations. But once the bases were built, the permanent jobs there were few and menial, and the bulk of the native population lived in poverty. After the war, the region retained its strategic importance. In 1955 many Eskimos were again employed temporarily, this time to construct the Distant Early Warning line, a network of radar posts that stretched across the Arctic from Alaska to Baffin Island.

Nowhere in the Far North was the impact of the war and its aftermath more pronounced than in Greenland, which remained a possession of Denmark, having been recolonized by Danes a few centuries after the Norse settlements failed. Disturbed by the spread of disease and alcoholism, the Danish government had issued a charter in the late 18th century designed to insulate the island's indigenous population from corrupting influences. As a consequence, whites from ships and trading posts could visit Eskimos only with the permission of local authorities. In 1921 Denmark closed the coast of Greenland to all but its own citizens. But when Denmark was subsequently occupied by Nazi Germany during World War II and cut off from its New World colony, the United States took over the defense of the island. The American military presence during the war and after, when an enormous air base was constructed at Thule, opened up Greenland to the world.

Thus the Eskimos of Greenland were thrust into the modern era—a transition that indigenous peoples were undergoing with varying degrees of success all across the frozen North. By conventional measures, the standard of living improved for many native families as a result. By the late 1960s, a number of them lived in modern frame houses—often government subsidized—in permanent year-round villages. Many communities had electricity, running water, and an airstrip to link them with the outside world. Public schools were replacing those run by missionaries, as the governments of the United States, Canada, and Denmark assumed greater responsibility for preparing Eskimos for the modern world.

Two Yupik men from Scammon Bay, Alaska, one of them wearing a grass mask to filter the smoke, enjoy a sweat bath together. Sweat baths are still taken for ritual pu-rification as well as for pleasure.

But such improvements often came grudgingly, and serious problems remained. Native Alaskans, for example, were required to send their high school students to distant boarding schools until a court consent decree issued in 1976 mandated a secondary school in any village requesting one. In many communities, the cost of electricity remained prohibitively high for Eskimos who depended largely on government welfare. Public health services reduced the incidence of disease and cut infant mortality rates. But many native northerners still used buckets for toilets and de-rived their drinking water from melted ice and snow—conditions that gave rise to epidemics of hepatitis.

Even people whose material conditions improved significantly as a result of modernization had to cope with the continued erosion of their traditions. Hunting and fishing remained the heart and soul of native cul-ture. But living off the land became increasingly difficult. Many of the old skills were lost as boys sought jobs or went to school instead of accompa-nying their elders on hunting expeditions. And those who ventured out to hunt on weekends increasingly made use of purchased technology. Boats of aluminum or fiberglass took the place of the skin-covered umiaks and kayaks; gasoline engines supplanted paddles and oars, except in certain areas of Greenland where motorboats were banned in hunting seals and whales. And dog teams began to give way to snowmobiles, which were

CONTESTS OF STRENGTH AND DEXTERITY

Every July men and women from all over Alaska gather in Fairbanks to participate in the World Eskimo-Indian Olympics. Founded in 1961, the four-day-long sports festival features ancient games that test endurance, agility, strength, and other qualities needed for survival in rural regions even today. The event is also an opportunity for the diverse native communities of Alaska to gather as one and celebrate their shared heritage. For city dwellers especially, the Olympics are a vital link to traditional culture. "In Anchorage we don't have whaling festivals or potlatches," explained one urbanite. "We don't have the same celebrations people in villages have. We need the games as a yearly celebration of who we are, why we are."

Until about a decade ago, the games were informal and loosely organized. When the master of ceremonies announced the start of an event, young spectators with no special training came down from the bleachers to compete. Now athletes train all winter, perfecting their skills and, in the process, setting higher standards. Although the games have gotten tougher, the spirit of cooperation rather than competition prevails. "Your competitor is your greatest supporter in native games," said one athlete. "That's not the feeling you get playing basketball or other white men's games. I was taught a kind of native law of life; if you wish the worst for your competitor, it's just going to come back at you. If you give your competitor confidence and support, that spirit will come back to you, too."

At the opening of the 1988 World Eskimo-Indian Olympics, two officials light sticks from a torch held by two athletes. The sticks will be used to ignite a ceremonial seal-oil lamp that will burn throughout the games.

An athlete sails to the ceiling during the Blanket Toss. Participants in this test of timing and balance must not look down while airborne and must remain upright when they hit the walrushide blanket.

A competitor displays stamina during **Drop the Bomb.** He must keep his body in a rigid cross while helpers carry him as far as they can before he "drops the bomb," or sags from exhaustion.

During the **Ear Weight** contest, a man carries 16 pounds of lead on a piece of twine looped over one ear. He must walk around, hands behind his back, until he drops the weights or until they fall from his ear.

During the **One-Hand Reach,** a young man balances his body on one hand while straining to tap a sealskin ball suspended above him—a test of balance and strength.

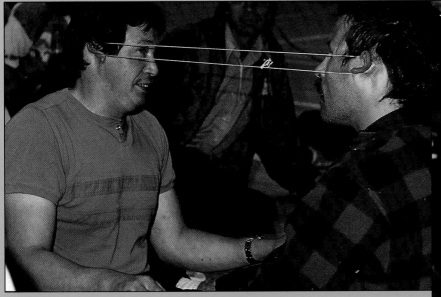

Sinew looped around their ears, men struggle in a painful tug of war— the Ear Pull. One loses if the sinew slips from his ear.

Performing the High Kick, a girl balances on one hand, holds a foot with the other, and uses her free foot to kick a ball hanging above her.

A competitor bounces across the floor on his knuckles during the Knuckle Hop, which calls for contestants to imitate a seal climbing onto ice floes. This grueling endurance test is always the last game of the Olympics because of the damage it inflicts upon contestants' hands.

not always reliable but could pull a sled up to three times faster and did not have to be fed and cared for, or laboriously harnessed and lashed.

Eskimos increasingly found themselves hemmed in by strict government wildlife regulations that were designed to preserve natural resources. Such laws made little sense to a people who had always honored the spirits of the animals and never taken more than they needed. Dismayed by a 1985 whaling quota, one native Alaskan complained, "How can we teach our children to be whalers if we are only permitted to take our boats out on only four strikes?"

In the political arena, Eskimos in recent decades have struggled for their territorial rights with a fighting spirit reminiscent of their ancestors. The question of native claims came to a head in the western Arctic after

Lights from paraffin lamps shine from the wooden houses of Moriussaq, a modern Inuit village in northern Greenland. Each home has its own shed equipped with racks for storing fuel, sleds, and frozen meat and fish.

Wrapped in walrus skin in the traditional manner, these packets of meat and blubber are ready for storage in a permafrost cache. The packets will remain edible for as long as a year.

the discovery in 1968 of huge oil reserves beneath Prudhoe Bay on Alaska's north coast. The following year, the state of Alaska earned $900 million in one day by auctioning off drilling concessions. Drilling for oil and natural gas soon extended eastward into the realm of Canadian Eskimos.

Although petroleum development posed potential threats to the arctic environment and the traditional culture, it also presented an opportunity for native Alaskans—Indians as well as Eskimos and Aleuts—to push for recognition of their land rights. When Alaska became a state in 1959, authorities allowed the state to select 104 million acres of prime land to be part of its public domain. Much of this territory had been traditionally used or occupied by Eskimos, but local and federal authorities ignored their claims. A decade later, with the Prudhoe Bay find, native Alaskans tried again, this time backed by oil companies that needed to settle the matter in order to build a $10 billion pipeline to carry crude oil nearly 800 miles from there to the little port of Valdez on Alaska's southeastern coast.

Native rights were finally recognized legally in 1971 when the U.S. Congress approved the Alaska Native Claims Settlement Act. Alaskans of one-fourth or more native ancestry were granted ownership of 12 percent of the state's territory—44 million acres—and offered $962.5 million for relinquishing rights to the remaining land. Individuals did not receive the land and money directly but became shareholders in regional and village corporations mandated by the legislation. These corporations invested the government payments in enterprises ranging from fish-processing plants and pipeline maintenance firms to hotel management companies. Hampered by a lack of management experience and drained by legal and administrative expenses, the majority of the corporations were able to produce little profit for their shareholders.

Fearing that they might lose what they had gained in the way of self-determination if the tribal corporations faltered, native Alaskans pressed for a measure of political autonomy. In 1973 six northern towns elected to become a single self-governing entity known as the North Slope Borough. One of the borough's first steps was to tax land owned by the oil companies. The revenue raised was used to modernize existing houses, schools, and health clinics and to construct new ones. In 1983 a similar urge to assert their sovereignty prompted several tribal governments in southwestern Alaska to band together to form the self-proclaimed Yupiit Nation. Such homegrown movements have not assumed all the powers exercised by the state and federal governments. Through political pressure, however, they have sought to strengthen native hunting and fishing rights and to alleviate social problems, including chronic unemployment, inadequate education, and high rates of domestic violence, alcoholism, and suicide.

The recent political resurgence in Alaska has been accompanied by a cultural revival. Thanks to the requirements for proving eligibility under the Alaska Native Claims Settlement Act, identity as a native—Eskimo, Aleut, or Indian—became a sought-after status. People of mixed ancestry now saw their native background as an asset and encouraged their children to take pride in the age-old traditions. Eskimos who were familiar with the old ways worked to preserve them. They revived traditional dances and ceremonies once prohibited by missionaries. And they set up camps where youngsters flocked to learn the ancient survival skills.

In 1979 the people of Greenland—most of them of mixed Eskimo and European descent—won home rule from Denmark, gaining the right to regulate taxes, fisheries, hunting, agriculture, labor, education, and health. Denmark still controlled foreign policy, the police, and the judiciary, but the changes were a major step toward possible national independence.

Nowhere was the struggle for self-determination more dramatic—or more prolonged—than in Canada. The Inuit Tapirisat, or Brotherhood, was organized in 1971, the same year that their brethren in neighboring Alaska won recognition of their ancient land claims. The Brotherhood sought redress not only for their own neglected land claims but also for other grievances such as the forced relocation of some of their people during the 1950s. Beginning in 1953, the Canadian government had ordered the transfer of Inuit families from northern Quebec to two new settlements more than 1,000 miles away in the Far North—Resolute Bay on Cornwallis Island and Grise Fiord on Ellesmere Island. The government rationalized the move as an attempt to increase hunting opportunities for the emigrants. "It was like landing on the moon," recalled John Amagoalik, an unwilling participant in the forced relocation and later president of the Brotherhood. "There was absolutely nothing but gray gravel and snow." He was six years old when the government deposited his family on the

Driving snowmo-biles towing sleds laden with game, Yupik seal hunters head home to Tu-nunak, Alaska. Throughout the Arc-tic, snowmobiles have replaced dogs as the principal means of trans-portation—a revolu-tion in mobility that rivals the rifle's im-pact on hunting.

rocky, wind-swept beaches of southern Ellesmere Island. They had only tents for shelter and little equipment to cope with life in one of the world's harshest environments, where temperatures plunged to 60 degrees below zero. Their settlement, only 900 miles from the North Pole, was the north-ernmost in North America.

In January 1992, the Brotherhood finally won a formal apology from the Canadian government, but that was only the beginning. Under pres-sure from Amagoalik and other Inuits, the government settled the land claims with a momentous concession—a promise to create a new Inuit-dominated territory, effective in 1999. It will be carved from the old North-west Territories and will include most of the Arctic Archipelago between Alaska and Greenland, encompassing a total of 772,000 square miles, an area larger than Alaska and California combined. As part of the settle-ment, the Inuit, who will make up 80 percent of the territory's 22,000 citi-zens, will receive $1.15 billion. In addition, they will hold title to 136,530 square miles, or about 18 percent of the territory, and control subsurface rights to oil, gas, and minerals on nearly 10 percent of this land. Unlike the Alaskans, whose claims settlement lacked such a clause, they will be able to hunt, fish, and trap for "basic needs" anywhere in the territory without restriction. This provision for subsistence as an officially recognized way of life after more than four centuries of outside intervention makes the name of the new territory even more appropriate. It will be known as Nunavut, which in the language of the Inuit means Our Land.

THE ART OF IVORY CARVING

For more than 2,000 years, Eskimo men have taught their sons two skills vital to survival in their harsh homeland: how to hunt animals and how to carve ivory. Indeed, in traditional Eskimo culture, carving was considered as important as hunting, for without it there would have been no weapons with which to kill game, nor many of the other tools that enabled the people of the North to thrive in their polar clime.

Using the prized ivory tusks of the walrus—and sometimes ancient mammoth or mastodon tusks that they had scavenged from the beach or tundra—Eskimo men fashioned not only their own hunting equipment but also the everyday household implements used by their wives and families. These hunter-carvers strove to make their handiwork as beautiful as it was functional. Working painstakingly, they sculpted tools into pleasing shapes and often incised surfaces with decorations inspired by Eskimo religious beliefs. The exquisite engravings found on many weapons and amulets, for example, were intended to honor and entice animal spirits and thus ensure an abundance of game. Geometric designs, as well as images of game animals and mythological creatures, adorned all manner of utensils, from snow goggles to needle cases.

Until the late 19th century, Eskimo carvers carried on much as their ancestors had. With the increasing presence of whalers, miners, and finally tourists in the arctic region, however, the ancient tradition—like many other of the Eskimos' old ways—underwent radical change. Realizing the possibilities for trade, the versatile carvers turned their skills to items that appealed to outsiders' tastes. So-called market art—cribbage boards, napkin rings, and myriad themes alien to Eskimo culture—soon dominated the ivory carver's repertoire.

Despite the increasing rarity of ivory, carving remains a strong cultural tradition. In recent decades, many carvers—including a few women now—have reclaimed traditional themes with works such as small animal sculptures. A number of Eskimos, moreover, have emerged as professional artists. Interestingly, traditional Eskimo languages have no word for "art." Nevertheless, no other term does justice to the extraordinary ivory objects, created by carvers past and present, that appear here and on the following pages.

The mouthpiece of a bow drill held between his teeth, a 19th-century Eskimo sculpts a chunk of raw ivory. Propelled by a bow made of thong and bone, the mouthpiece drill gives the carver one free hand to manipulate the object being carved.

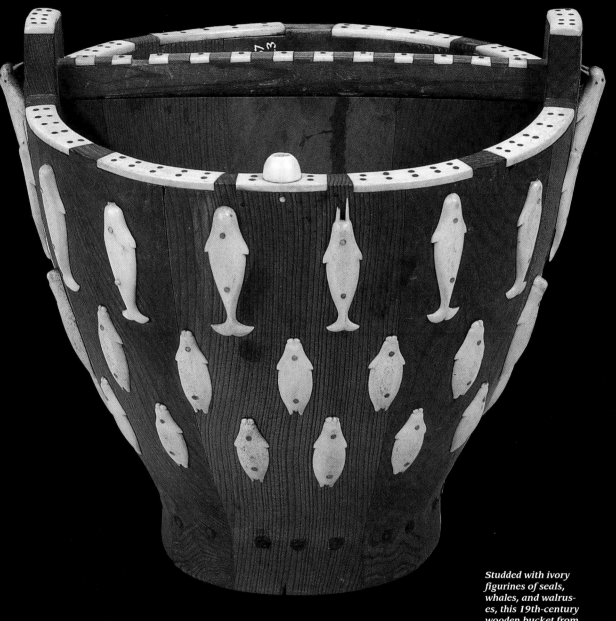

Studded with ivory figurines of seals, whales, and walruses, this 19th-century wooden bucket from Greenland is a stunning example of the Eskimo carver's ability to transform ordinary utensils into objects of extraordinary beauty.

THE HUNTER'S GEAR

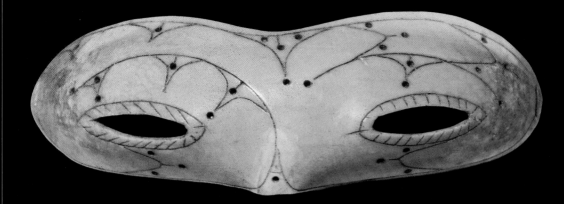

Flowing asymmetrical designs adorn this antique pair of ivory goggles, worn to shield the hunter's eyes from the blinding glare of the arctic snow cover.

Designed to pierce thick skin and blubber, a harpoon point is set in a heavy socket piece engraved to resemble a wolf—perhaps in order to invoke lupine hunting prowess.

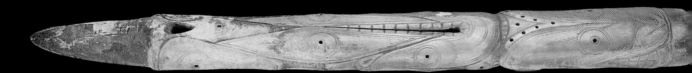

Graceful curvilinear markings—which may symbolize spirit helpers—embellish this 1,000-year-old spearpoint from the Bering Sea region.

Used by a hunter to gain speed and distance as he hurled his spear, this wooden throwing stick is ornamented with small ivory seals in honor of this important game animal.

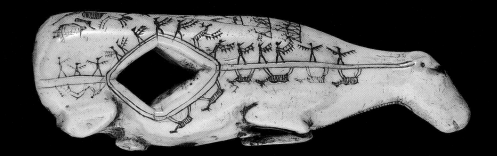

Images of the legendary Thunderbird are used to decorate this bear-shaped arrow straightener, which worked as a lever to align bent wooden shafts.

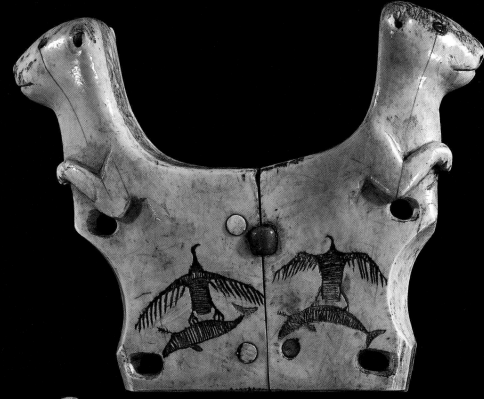

Affixed to the prow of a kayak as a cradle for a hunter's weapon, this harpoon rest branches into twin polar bear heads. Engravings of Thunderbirds clutching whales in their talons also decorate the tool, perhaps to imbue the harpoon with the power of the great winged hunter.

TOOLS FOR WOMEN'S WORK

Two ivory thread spools reflect the imagination of individual craftsmen: The top spool is carved in the likeness of a seal; the bottom features a legendary mermaid creature, with the head and arms of a woman joined to the flippers of a walrus.

Topped by a bear's head, this sinuous ivory rod is a boot sole creaser—a common household implement employed to maintain the shape of the heels and toes of boots.

Used to crush lice removed during routine grooming, this utilitarian device is whimsically shaped as a four-toed foot.

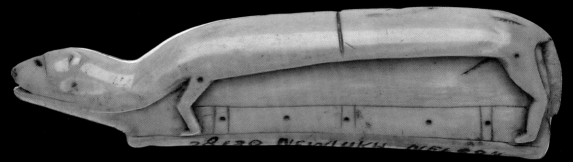

Slim and elongated, an ivory polar bear forms the handle of this utility knife. Knives such as these were used for skinning and cutting up fish and game.

Flanked by seals, a frowning woman and a smiling man—symbols of balance and harmony when depicted together—decorate opposite sides of a bag fastener. The device is used to secure the small skin bag, known as a "housewife," in which Eskimo women store their tools.

CREATIONS FOR THE OUTSIDE MARKET

Embellished with many real and fanciful creatures, this exquisitely crafted cribbage board—used for scorekeeping in a popular card game—retains the curve of the walrus tusk from which it was carved.

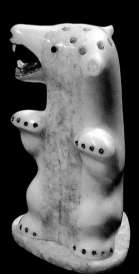

The mottled core of the walrus tusk is evident in this pair of salt and pepper shakers shaped like bears. Shakers that were modeled after animals became popular souvenirs during the 1930s.

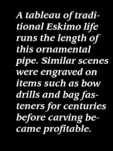

A tableau of traditional Eskimo life runs the length of this ornamental pipe. Similar scenes were engraved on items such as bow drills and bag fasteners for centuries before carving became profitable.

Complete with sails and rigging but devoid of Eskimo motifs, this whaling ship model reflects the versatility of the Eskimo carver. Models such as these were in great demand at the turn of the 20th century.

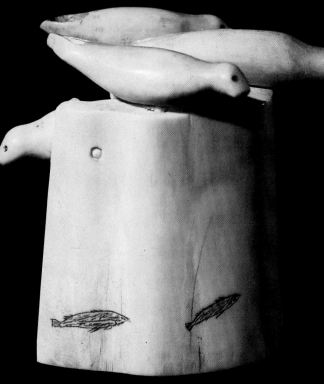

Sleek and smooth, the seals in this sculpture capture the essence of the animal in true Eskimo style. Two fish engraved at the base of the seals' perch—fashioned from a section of walrus tusk—indicate the water below.

OLD THEMES FOR MODERN CARVERS

A contemporary ivory carver on Little Diomede Island remains true to his roots by using a hand-powered bow drill similar to those that were employed by his ancestors.

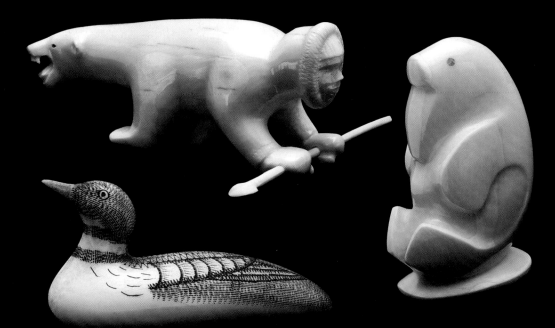

Ivory miniatures— such as the finely feathered loon (far left, bottom) and the walrus (left), are a specialty of modern carvers. Another common theme is the representation of traditional stories such as the transformation of a man into a polar bear (far left, top).

Laden with gear, a hunter drags his kill behind him in this sculpture by a Greenland artist. Although the piece is contemporary, it reflects the traditional Eskimo carver's style of portraying animals more realistically than humans.

ACKNOWLEDGMENTS

The editors wish to thank the following individuals and institutions for their valuable assistance in the preparation of this volume:

In Canada:
Manitoba—Margot Rousset, Winnipeg Art Gallery, Winnipeg. Northwest Territories—Larry Pontus, Government of the Northwest Territories, Department of Justice, Yellowknife. Quebec—Margery Toner, Canadian Museum of Civilization, Hull.

In Denmark:
Copenhagen—Rolf Gilberg, Department of Ethnography, The National Museum of Denmark.

In England:
Cambridge—Robert Headland. London—Jim Hamill, Phillip Taylor.

In the United States:
Alaska: Anaktuvuk Pass—Simon Paneak Memorial Museum. Anchorage—Diane Brenner, Mina Jacobs, Anchorage Museum of History and Art; Chris Wooley. Barrow—Johnny Adams, Karen Brewster, Janna Harcharak, North Slope Borough. Fairbanks—Marge Heath, Gretchen Lake, Elmer E. Rasmuson Library, University of Alaska. Juneau—Gladi Kulp, India Spartz, Alaska State Library; Steve Henrikson, Alaska State Museum; Phyllis Bradner, Division of Tourism; Lynn Ager Wallen. Wasilla—Bill Hess, Running Dog Publications.
Oregon: Eugene—Don E. Dumond, Department of Anthropology, University of Oregon.
Washington, D.C.: William W. Fitzhugh, Arctic Studies Center, Felicia Pickering, Department of Anthropology, Smithsonian Institution.
Washington State: Port Townsend—Dorothy Jean Ray. Seattle—Rebecca Andrews, Robin K. Wright, The Burke Museum; Mardonna Austin-McKillip, The Legacy, Ltd.; Richard H. Engeman, Sandra Kroupa, John Medlin, Gary L. Menges, Carla Rickerson, University of Washington Libraries; Sari Ott, Stan Shockey, University of Washington.

BIBLIOGRAPHY

Alexander, Bryan, and Cherry Alexander, *The Eskimos.* New York: Crescent Books, 1991.
America's Fascinating Indian Heritage. Pleasantville, New York: Reader's Digest Association, 1990.
Balikci, Asen, *The Netsilik Eskimo.* Garden City, New York: Natural History Press, 1970.
Barker, James H., *Always Getting Ready Upterrlainarluta: Yup'ik Eskimo Subsistence in Southwest Alaska.* Seattle: University of Washington Press, 1993.
Beck, Peggy V., Anna Lee Walters, and Nia Francisco, *The Sacred: Ways of Knowledge, Sources of Life.* Tsaile, Arizona: Navajo Community College Press, 1992.
Berger, Thomas R., *Village Journey: The Report of the Alaska Native Review Commission.* New York: Hill and Wang, 1985.
Black, Lydia T., *Aleut Art: Unangam Aguqaadangin Unangan of the Aleutian Archipelago.* Anchorage: Aleutian/Pribilof Islands Association, 1982.
Boas, Franz, *The Central Eskimo.* Lincoln: University of Nebraska Press, 1964.
Briggs, Jean L., *Never in Anger: Portrait of an Eskimo Family.* Cambridge, Massachusetts: Harvard University Press, 1970.
Bringle, Mary, *Eskimos.* New York: Franklin Watts, 1973.
Brody, Hugh, *Living Arctic: Hunters of the Canadian North.* Seattle: University of Washington Press, 1990.

Bruemmer, Fred, *Seasons of the Eskimo: A Vanishing Way of Life.* Greenwich, Connecticut: New York Graphic Society, 1971.
Burch, Ernest S., Jr.:
The Eskimos: Echoes of the Ancient World. Norman: University of Oklahoma Press, 1988.
Eskimo Kinsmen: Changing Family Relationships in Northwest Alaska. St. Paul, Minnesota: West Publishing, 1975.
Carpenter, Edmund, *Eskimo Realities.* New York: Holt, Rinehart and Winston, 1973.
Cellura, Dominique, *Travelers of the Cold: Sled Dogs of the Far North.* Anchorage: Alaska Northwest Books, 1990.
Collins, Henry B., et al., *The Far North: 2,000 Years of American Eskimo and Indian Art.* Bloomington: Indiana University Press, 1977.
Condon, Richard G., *Inuit Behavior and Seasonal Change in the Canadian Arctic.* Ann Arbor, Michigan: UMI Research Press, 1983.
Coppinger, Lorna, and The International Sled Dog Racing Association, *The World of Sled Dogs: From Siberia to Sport Racing.* New York: Howell Book House, 1977.
Damas, David, ed., *Arctic.* Vol. 5 of *Handbook of North American Indians.* Washington, D.C.: Smithsonian Institution, 1984.
Driver, Harold E., *Indians of North America.* Chicago: University of Chicago Press, 1969.
Dumond, Don E., *The Eskimos and Aleuts.* London: Thames and Hudson, 1987.
Fienup-Riordan, Ann:

Eskimo Essays: Yup'ik Lives and How We See Them. New Brunswick, New Jersey: Rutgers University Press, 1990.
The Nelson Island Eskimo: Social Structure and Ritual Distribution. Anchorage: Alaska Pacific University Press, 1983.
Fitzhugh, William W., and Aron Crowell, *Crossroads of Continents: Cultures of Siberia and Alaska.* Washington, D.C.: Smithsonian Institution Press, 1988.
Fitzhugh, William W., and Susan A. Kaplan, *Inua: Spirit World of the Bering Sea Eskimo.* Washington, D.C.: Smithsonian Institution Press, 1982.
Foulks, Edward F., *The Arctic Hysterias of the North Alaskan Eskimo.* Washington, D.C.: American Anthropological Association, 1972.
Freuchen, Peter, *Book of the Eskimos.* Ed. by Dagmar Freuchen. Cleveland, Ohio: World Publishing, 1961.
Furst, Peter T., and Jill L. Furst, *North American Indian Art.* New York: Rizzoli, 1982.
Fury of the Northmen, by the Editors of Time-Life Books (Time Frame series). Alexandria, Virginia: Time-Life Books, 1988.
Graburn, Nelson H. H., *Eskimos without Igloos: Social and Economic Development in Sugluk.* Boston: Little, Brown, 1969.
Grzimek's Encyclopedia of Mammals. Vols. 1-5. New York: McGraw-Hill, 1990.
Harper, Kenn, *Give Me My Father's Body: The Life of Minik, the New York Eskimo.* Frobisher Bay, Northwest Territories: Blacklead Books, 1986.

Hart Hansen, Jens Peder, Jorgen Meldgaard, and Jorgen Nordqvist, eds., *The Greenland Mummies.* Washington, D.C.: Smithsonian Institution Press, 1991.

Hawkes, Ernest William, *The Labrador Eskimo.* New York: Johnson Reprint, 1970 (reprint of 1916 edition).

Herbert, Wally, *Eskimos.* New York: Franklin Watts, 1977.

Herbert, Wally, and the Editors of Time-Life Books, *Hunters of the Polar North: The Eskimos.* (Peoples of the Wild series). Amsterdam: Time-Life Books, 1981.

Hess, Bill:
A Gift from the Whales: A Photographer's Search for the Last Buffalo Hunt. Wasilla, Alaska: Running Dog Publications, 1993.
Kivgiq: A Photographic Celebration of the Messenger Feast. Wasilla, Alaska: Running Dog Publications, 1994.

Hoebel, E. Adamson, "Song Duels among the Eskimo." In *Law and Warfare: Studies in the Anthropology of Conflict.* Ed. by Paul Bohannan. Garden City, New York: Natural History Press, 1967.

Hoyt-Goldsmith, Diane, *Arctic Hunter.* New York: Holiday House, 1992.

Hughes, Jill, *Eskimos.* New York: Gloucester Press, 1978.

Humber, Charles J., ed., *Canada's Native Peoples.* Vol. 2 in *Canada Heirloom Series.* Mississauga, Ontario: Heirloom Publishing, 1988.

Jenness, Diamond, *The Life of the Copper Eskimos.* New York: Johnson Reprint, 1970.

Josephy, Alvin M., Jr., ed., *America in 1492: The World of the Indian Peoples before the Arrival of Columbus.* New York: Alfred A. Knopf, 1992.

Kaalund, Bodil, *The Art of Greenland: Sculpture, Crafts, Painting.* Transl. by Kenneth Tindall. Berkeley: University of California Press, 1983.

Kalman, Bobbie, and William Belsey, *An Arctic Community.* New York: Crabtree Publishing, 1988.

Keating, Bern, *Alaska.* Washington, D.C.: National Geographic Society, 1971.

Langdon, Steve J., *The Native People of Alaska.* Anchorage: Greatland Graphics, 1987.

Lantis, Margaret, *Alaskan Eskimo Ceremonialism.* New York: J. J. Augustin Publisher, 1947.

Lehane, Brendan, and the Editors of Time-Life Books, *The Northwest Passage.* (The Seafarers series). Alexandria, Virginia: Time-Life Books, 1981.

Lund, Annabel, and Mark Kelley, *Heartbeat: World Eskimo Indian Olympics.* Ed. by Howard Simons. Juneau, Alaska: Fairweather Press, 1986.

Merkur, Daniel, *Powers which We Do Not Know: The Gods and Spirits of the Inuit.* Moscow: University of Idaho Press, 1991.

Michael, Henry N., ed., *Lieutenant Zagoskin's Travels in Russian America, 1842-1844: The First Ethnographic and Geographic Investigations in the Yukon and Kuskokwim Valleys of Alaska.* Toronto: University of Toronto Press, 1967.

Morgan, Lael, *Art and Eskimo Power: The Life and Times of Alaskan Howard Rock.* Fairbanks, Alaska: Epicenter Press, 1988.

Morison, Samuel Eliot, *The Great Explorers: The European Discovery of America.* New York: Oxford University Press, 1978.

Nabokov, Peter, and Robert Easton, *Native American Architecture.* New York: Oxford University Press, 1989.

Nelson, Edward William, *The Eskimo about Bering Strait.* Washington, D.C.: Smithsonian Institution Press, 1983 (reprint of 1899 edition).

Nelson, Richard K., *Hunters of the Northern Ice.* Chicago: University of Chicago Press, 1969.

Osborn, Kevin, *The Peoples of the Arctic.* New York: Chelsea House Publishers, 1990.

Oswalt, Wendell H.:
Bashful No Longer. Norman: University of Oklahoma Press, 1990.
Eskimos and Explorers. Novato, California: Chandler & Sharp Publishers, 1979.

Parsons, Elsie Clews, ed., *American Indian Life.* New York: Greenwich House, 1983.

Peary, Robert E., *Northward over the "Great Ice": A Narrative of Life and Work along the Shores and upon the Interior Ice-Cap of Northern Greenland in the Years 1886 and 1891-1897.* Vol. 2. New York: Frederick A. Stokes, 1898.

Pisano, Beverly, *Siberian Huskies.* Neptune City, New Jersey: T. F. H. Publications, 1979.

Poncins, Gontran de, and Lewis Galantière, *Kabloona.* New York: Time Incorporated, 1965.

Rasmussen, Knud, *Across Arctic America: Narrative of the Fifth Thule Expedition.* New York: G. P. Putnam's Sons, 1927.

Ray, Dorothy Jean:
Aleut and Eskimo Art: Tradition and Innovation in South Alaska. Seattle: University of Washington Press, 1981.
Artists of the Tundra and the Sea. Seattle: University of Washington Press, 1961.
Eskimo Art: Tradition and Innovation in North Alaska. Seattle: University of Washington Press, 1977.
Eskimo Masks: Art and Ceremony. Seattle: University of Washington Press, 1987.

Riddle, Maxwell, and Beth J. Harris, *The New Complete Alaskan Malamute.* New York: Howell Book House, 1990.

Ridington, Robin, "Northern Hunters." In *America in 1492: The World of the Indian Peoples before the Arrival of Columbus.* Ed. by Alvin M. Josephy, Jr. New York: Alfred A. Knopf, 1992.

Ritchie, Carson I. A., *The Eskimo and His Art.* New York: St. Martin's Press, 1975.

Smith, J. G. E., *Arctic Art: Eskimo Ivory.* New York: Museum of the American Indian, 1980.

Spencer, Robert F., *The North Alaskan Eskimo: A Study in Ecology and Society.* Washington, D.C.: Smithsonian Institution Press, 1959.

Spencer, Robert F., et al., *The Native Americans.* New York: Harper & Row, 1977.

The Spirit Sings: Artistic Traditions of Canada's First Peoples. Toronto: McClelland and Stewart and Glenbow Museum, 1987.

Underhill, Ruth M., *Red Man's Religion: Beliefs and Practices of the Indians North of Mexico.* Chicago: University of Chicago Press, 1965.

Vanstone, James W., *Point Hope: An Eskimo Village in Transition.* Seattle: University of Washington Press, 1962.

Wardwell, Allen, *Ancient Eskimo Ivories of the Bering Strait.* New York: Hudson Hills Press, 1986.

The World of the American Indian. Washington, D.C.: National Geographic Society, 1989.

Yue, Charlotte, and David Yue, *The Igloo.* Boston: Houghton Mifflin, 1988.

Zimmerly, David W., *Qajaq: Kayaks of Siberia and Alaska.* Juneau: Alaska State Museum, 1986.

PERIODICALS

Ager, Lynn Price, "Storyknifing: An Alaskan Eskimo Girls' Game." *Journal of the Folklore Institute,* March 1975.

Beaulieu, Carole, "Between Hunting and Hard Rock." *World Press Review,* July 1992.

Bogojavlensky, Sergei, and Robert W. Fuller, "Polar Bears, Walrus Hides, and Social Solidarity." *The Alaska Journal,* Spring 1973.

Cernetig, Miro, "Nunavut Leaders in Short Supply." Toronto: *The Globe and Mail,* August 2, 1993.

Claiborne, William:
"Arctic Village Finds Old Way is Best: Rigorous Eskimo Traditions Serve as Defense against Social Ills." *The Washington Post,* April 17, 1992.
"Canada Admits Violating Rights of Inuit People." *The Washington Post,* January 16, 1992.
"Eskimos Hail Step toward Homeland: Plan to Split Northwest Territories Narrowly Approved at Polls." *The Washington Post,* May 6, 1992.

Force, Roland W., "Arctic Art: Eskimo Ivory." *American Indian Art Magazine,* Spring 1981.

Hess, Bill:
"Barrow Hosts Give Warm Welcome to All." *Uiñiq: The Open Lead,* May 1990.
"A Gift From the Whales." *Running Dog Magazine,* September, 1990.
"Kivgiq-Looking Back in Hope of a Better Future." *Uiñiq: The Open Lead,* Summer 1988.

Pelly, David F., "Dawn of Nunavut." *Canadian Geographic,* March/April 1993.

Ray, Dorothy Jean, "Happy Jack: King of the Eskimo Ivory Carvers." *American Indian Art Magazine,* Winter 1984.

Reimer, Holly F., "World Eskimo-Indian Olympics." *Native Peoples,* Fall 1991.

Reynolds, Brad, "Eskimo Hunters of the Bering Sea." *National Geographic,* June 1984.

Zellen, Barry, "Risks and Promises in the New North." Toronto: *The Globe and Mail,* May 28, 1993.

OTHER PUBLICATIONS

"The AFN Report on the Status of Alaska Natives: A Call for Action." Anchorage: Alaska Federation of Natives, January 1989.

The Coming and Going of the Shaman: Eskimo Shamanism and Art. Winnipeg, Manitoba: Winnipeg Art Gallery, 1979.

Oswalt, Wendell H., "Traditional Storyknife Tales of Yuk Girls." *Proceedings of the American Philosophical Society.* Philadelphia: American Philosophical Society, 1964.

Rainey, Froelich G., "The Whale Hunters of Tigara." *Anthropological Papers of the American Museum of Natural History,* Vol. 41, Part 2. New York: American Museum of Natural History, 1952.

Sivunniigvik (the Planning Place). Kotzebue, Alaska: NANA Museum of the Arctic, 1985.

Thalbitzer, William, "The Heathen Priests of East Greenland (Angakut)." *Proceedings of the 16th International Congress of Americanists,* Vienna, 1908.

PICTURE CREDITS

The sources for the illustrations that appear in this book are listed below. Credits from left to right are separated by semicolons; from top to bottom they are separated by dashes.

Cover: © Jack Elness/Comstock, Inc. **6, 7:** Background Bruno P. Zehnder, Peter Arnold, Inc. Western History Collections, University of Oklahoma Library; Fred Hirschmann, Wasilla, Alaska. **8, 9:** Background Bios (Klein-Hubert), Peter Arnold, Inc. Western History Collections, University of Oklahoma Library; © John Eastcott/Yva Momatiuk. **10, 11:** Background Tim Thompson, Bainbridge Island, Washington. Richard Harrington/National Archives of Canada/PA-129026; © John Eastcott/Yva Momatiuk. **12, 13:** Background Bruno P. Zehnder, Peter Arnold, Inc. Western History Collections, University of Oklahoma Library; George F. Mobley, © National Geographic Society. **14, 15:** Background Fred Bruemmer, Peter Arnold, Inc. Western History Collections, University of Oklahoma Library; © John Eastcott/Yva Momatiuk. **16, 17:** Background © Momatiuk/Eastcott/Woodfin Camp and Associates. Anchorage Museum Archives of History; Bryan and Cherry Alexander, Sturminster Newton, Dorset. **18, 19:** Larry Sherer, Department of Anthropology, Smithsonian Institution, cat. no. 45060—Bryan and Cherry Alexander, Sturminster Newton, Dorset/copyright 1981, Time-Life Books B.V. **21:** Tom Bean. **22:** Lomen Family Collection, Alaska and Polar Regions Department, University of Alaska, Fairbanks, acc. no. 72-71-786N. **23:** Smithsonian Institution, National Museum of Natural History (NMNH), Arctic Studies Center. **24, 25:** Maryland CartoGraphics, Inc. **26, 27:** Photography by Chlaus Lotscher, Homer, Alaska. **28, 29:** Fred Bruemmer; Bryan and Cherry Alexander, Sturminster Newton, Dorset; The National Museum of Denmark, Department of Ethnography, photo by Kit Weiss. **30-33:** Bryan and Cherry Alexander, Sturminster Newton, Dorset. **36:** Bryan and Cherry Alexander, Sturminster Newton, Dorset/copyright 1981, Time-Life Books B.V. **37:** Smithsonian Institution, NMNH, Arctic Studies Center, neg. no. 83-10709. **38, 39:** Bryan and Cherry Alexander, Sturminster Newton, Dorset/copyright 1981, Time-Life Books B.V. **40:** Smithsonian Institution, NMNH, Arctic Studies Center. **41:** Alaska State Museum, Juneau. **42:** Smithsonian Institution, NMNH, Arctic Studies Center—Alaska State Museum, Juneau. **45:** © John Eastcott/Yva Momatiuk. **46:** Bryan and Cherry Alexander, Sturminster Newton, Dorset/copyright 1981, Time-Life Books B.V. **47:** Greenland National Museum and Archives, Nuuk—Bryan and Cherry Alexander, Sturminster Newton, Dorset/copyright 1981, Time-Life Books B.V. **49, 50:** Bryan and Cherry Alexander, Sturminster Newton, Dorset. **51:** Peter T. Furst. **52:** Bryan and Cherry Alexander, Sturminster Newton, Dorset. **54, 55:** © Momatiuk/Eastcott/Woodfin Camp and Associates. **56, 57:** Tim Thompson, Bainbridge Island, Washington—© John Eastcott/Yva Momatiuk. **58, 59:** Bryan and Cherry Alexander, Sturminster Newton, Dorset/copyright 1981, Time-Life Books B.V. **60, 61:** Smithsonian Institution, neg. no. 80-16583; neg. no. NAA-6924. **62, 63:** Bryan and Cherry

Alexander, Sturminster Newton, Dorset/copyright 1981, Time-Life Books B.V. **64, 65:** Bryan and Cherry Alexander, Sturminster Newton, Dorset (2); Bryan and Cherry Alexander, Sturminster Newton, Dorset/copyright 1981, Time-Life Books B.V. **66-69:** Bryan and Cherry Alexander, Sturminster Newton, Dorset/copyright 1981, Time-Life Books B.V. **70, 71:** Bryan and Cherry Alexander, Sturminster Newton, Dorset; Bryan and Cherry Alexander, Sturminster Newton, Dorset/copyright 1981, Time-Life Books B.V. **72-81:** © Bill Hess. **82:** Library of Congress, neg. no. USZ62-101338. **84:** From *Northward Over the Great Ice* by Robert E. Peary, Frederick Strokes Co., N.Y., 1898. **85:** Smithsonian Institution, NMNH, Arctic Studies Center. **87:** Alex Harris, Archive Pictures Inc. **88, 89:** Art by Bobbi Tull. **90:** Larry Sherer, Department of Anthropology, NMNH; Smithsonian Institution, cat. no. 44998. **91:** National Museum of the American Indian (NMAI), Smithsonian Institution, neg. no. 4/9236. **92:** Bryan and Cherry Alexander, Sturminster Newton, Dorset—National Museum of American History, Smithsonian Institution, cat. no. 80-16591. **93:** Bryan and Cherry Alexander, Sturminster Newton, Dorset. **94:** Eric Freedman/Bruce Coleman, Inc.—Smithsonian Institution, NMNH, Arctic Studies Center. **95:** National Museum of American History, Smithsonian Institution, cat. no. 260-327—cat. no. 38-642. **97:** Peabody and Essex Museum, Salem, Mass., photo by Mark Sexton—courtesy Lynn Ager Wallen. **98, 99:** © John Eastcott/Yva Momatiuk. **100:** Canadian Museum of Civilization, neg. no. 42535. **101:** © John Eastcott/Yva Momatiuk. **102:** Library of Congress, neg. no. USZ262-101193. **103:** Michigan State University Archives & Historical Collections; Jim Brandenburg/Minden Pictures. **104, 105:** Smithsonian Institution, NMNH, Arctic Studies Center—James Balog/Bruce Coleman, Inc.; Smithsonian Institution, NMNH, Arctic Studies Center (2); courtesy Thomas Burke Memorial Washington State Museum, cat. no. 2-1233. **106:** © James H. Barker. **107:** Courtesy Trustees of the British Museum, London. **109:** Bryan and Cherry Alexander, Sturminster Newton, Dorset. **110:** The Royal Library, Copenhagen. **111:** Copyright British Museum, London. **112:** Smithsonian Institution, National Anthropological Archives (NAA), neg. no. 94-4208. **113:** Smithsonian Institution, NMNH, Arctic Studies Center—Larry Sherer, Department of Anthropology, Smithsonian Institution, cat. no. 45452. **115:** Gerth Lyberth, Jacobshavn Museum (2); Werner Forman Archive, William Channing Collection—artist, Kaarali Andreassen, photographer, Hans Petersen/Statens Museum for Kunst, Copenhagen. **116:** Smithsonian Institution, NMNH, Arctic Studies Center. **117:** © James H. Barker. **118:** National Museum of American History, Smithsonian Institution, cat. no. 80-18021—Special Collections Division, University of Washington Libraries, photo by Viola Garfield, neg. no. M503—National Museum of Greenland, Nuuk. **121:** Collections of the Ethnographic Museum of the University of Oslo—Special Collections Division, University of Washington Libraries, photo by J. Thwaites, neg. no. 3151. **122:** Smithsonian Institution, NMNH, Arctic Studies Center—Collection of the Winnipeg Art Gallery, purchased through a grant from Imperial Oil Ltd., by Jessie Onark, "Flight of the Shaman." **123:** Neg. no.

3371, photo by P. Hollembeak, courtesy Department of Library Services, American Museum of Natural History—used with permission of the Mystic Seaport Museum, Inc. **124, 125:** Ernest Mayer, Winnipeg Art Gallery (2)—Werner Forman Archive, London/American Museum of Natural History—Canadian Museum of Civilization, CMC no. S91-952. **126:** Phoebe A. Hearst Museum of Anthropology, University of California at Berkeley—used with permission of the Mystic Seaport Museum, Inc. **127:** Sheldon Jackson Museum—used with permission of the Mystic Seaport Museum, Inc. **128, 129:** Smithsonian Institution, NMNH, Arctic Studies Center. **130:** Peter T. Furst. **131:** NMAI, Smithsonian Institution, neg. no. 9/3432. **132, 133:** Courtesy Thomas Burke Memorial Washington State Museum, cat. no. 2-2128; Smithsonian Institution, NMNH, Arctic Studies Center. **134, 135:** Peter T. Furst; Smithsonian Institution, NMNH, Arctic Studies Center. **136, 137:** Peter T. Furst; Hamburgisches Museum für Völkerkunde. **138-141:** The National Museum of Denmark, Department of Ethnography, photo by Kit Weiss. **143:** Herzog Anton Ulrich-Museum, Braunschweig—courtesy Department of Library Services, American Museum of Natural History, neg. no. 220545. **146:** Scott Polar Research Institute, Cambridge, England, no. 66/3/47. **147:** Scott Polar Research Institute, Cambridge, England, no. 66/3/66; no. 66/3/75—no. 66/3/72—no. 66/3/65. **150:** Messenger Stick by Justus Mekiana, Anaktuvuk Pass, Alaska. **151-155:** © Bill Hess. **157:** Werner Forman Archive/Museum of Mankind, London—Bryan and Cherry Alexander, Sturminster Newton, Dorset. **159:** Lawrence Migdale. **160, 161:** © Bill Hess. **162:** James H. Barker. **163:** Bryan and Cherry Alexander, Sturminster Newton, Dorset. **164, 165:** Glenbow Archives, Calgary, Alberta—Smithsonian Archives, NAA. **167:** James H. Barker. **168:** Wayne Attla, Fairbanks, Alaska. **169:** Shultz/SIPA Press. **170:** Wayne Attla, Fairbanks, Alaska—SIPA Press/Rob Stapleton/Dembinsky Photo Associates, Owosso, Mich. **171:** Shultz/SIPA Press—Rob Stapleton/Dembinsky Photo Associates, Owosso, Mich.—Mark Kelley, Juneau, Alaska. **172, 173:** Bryan and Cherry Alexander, Sturminster Newton, Dorset/copyright 1981, Time-Life Books B.V.; photography by Chlaus Lotscher, Homer, Alaska. **175:** James H. Barker. **176:** Smithsonian Institution, neg. no.44826-B. **177:** Copyright British Museum, London. **178, 179:** Bobby Hansson, courtesy Gloria Manney Collection—Smithsonian Institution, NMNH, Arctic Studies Center (2)—copyright British Museum, London; copyright British Museum, London—Smithsonian Institution, neg. no. 81-2873. **180:** Smithsonian Institution, NMNH, Arctic Studies Center (3); Smithsonian Institution, no. 80-16601. **181:** Larry Sherer, Department of Anthropology, Smithsonian Institution, cat. no. 38129—Smithsonian Institution, NMNH, Arctic Studies Center (2). **182:** © Sisse Brimberg, 1983/Woodfin Camp and Associates—courtesy Jack and Layne Kleinart, Seattle—Smithsonian Institution, neg. no. 78-3039. **183:** Courtesy NMAI, Smithsonian Institution, neg. no. 21/4677—courtesy NMAI, Smithsonian Institution, no. 5/4317. **184, 185:** Fred Bruemmer/Peter Arnold, Inc.—Chris Arend, courtesy Anchorage Historical and Fine Arts Museum (3); Dave Marlow, Aspen.

INDEX